ABOUT THE AUTHOR

Stewart Wilde, a Sheffielder by birth, practised as an award-winning architect in the North of England and the London area for over 30 years before leaving the profession to concentrate on his interest in wine. Starting out in an off-licence and developing his knowledge through experience and examination he has now become increasingly, and especially, interested in the blossoming English and Welsh wine industry.

He has travelled widely in Western Europe, South America and New Zealand and has seen the emergence of 'at vineyard' hospitality in all these regions. He now concentrates on passing on that interest through talks, visits and this book. He lives with his wife Gill in South-West London. This is his second book on English and Welsh vineyards and their wines. His first book, *Sparkling Wine*, was published in 2019.

STEWART WILDE

Vineyard Vacations

In the Counties of England and Wales

AUSTIN MACAULEY PUBLISHERS™
LONDON • CAMBRIDGE • NEW YORK • SHARJAH

Copyright © Stewart Wilde 2023

The right of Stewart Wilde to be identified as author of this work has been asserted in accordance with section 77 and 78 of the Copyright, Designs and Patents Act 1988.

All rights reserved. No part of this publication may be reproduced, stored in a retrieval system, or transmitted in any form or by any means, electronic, mechanical, photocopying, recording, or otherwise, without the prior permission of the publishers.

Any person who commits any unauthorised act in relation to this publication may be liable to criminal prosecution and civil claims for damages.

A CIP catalogue record for this title is available from the British Library.

ISBN 9781398470408 (Paperback)
ISBN 9781398470415 (ePub e-book)

www.austinmacauley.com

First Published 2023
Austin Macauley Publishers Ltd
1 Canada Square
Canary Wharf
London
E14 5AA

DEDICATION

To my wife Gill for her support and understanding.

ACKNOWLEDGEMENTS

To Roger Cordwell, my early boss, friend and mentor.

To Trudy Welsh, AWE, DWSET, DLCI, my long-time friend and mentor.

To Julia Trustram Eve, WineGB, a long-time friend.

To all the included Vineyards for providing information and photographs.

Introduction

This book is not about wine, but about the places where wine can be found and where the visitor has somewhere to stay overnight. **The Vineyards**. Also all of the vineyards, included in this book, have some specific point of interest. This may be agricultural, oenological or historical. Agricultural would include their method of farming and planting. Oenological would be anything to do with their winemaking. Historical is about the vineyard, its owners and its location.

These selected vineyards can often be found in Areas of Outstanding Natural Beauty, in National Parks or at Sites of Special Scientific Interest and can offer an out of the way refuge with the benefit of home-produced wine. They may be large with comfortable accommodation or they may be small with basic facilities. In some instances they could be small and very luxurious. But they all have one thing in common and that is the welcome you receive when you choose to visit.

English Wine has a developing presence in the UK market place. However, not all of the vineyards, in what I would call the 'Winelands of England & Wales', are large enough to produce a sufficient quantity of wine to give them a presence on the high street outside their local area. To this end many of them wish to encourage visitors. In order to do this a number of vineyards have additional features to the wine that they produce and the guided tours and tutored tastings that they will have on offer. Many of them produce their own spirits of gin or brandy. They may also have their own brewery or apiary. Some of them have specialist features such as a Christmas tree plantation or having adventure pursuits facilities.

Within the 'Winelands of England & Wales' there are more than 70 such vineyards that offer the visitor an overnight stay overlooking, and often amongst, the vines. These added facilities may encourage more visitors to their area. These Winelands stretch from the Isles of Scilly, in the west, to the Kent coast, in the east, from the Isle of Wight, in the south, and the Yorkshire Wolds to the north and they can be found in most of the counties in between. The overnight accommodation offered can vary from serviced bare camp sites to bed and breakfast hotels. The bricks and mortar accommodation can be in converted listed farm buildings, sometime dating from the 18th century, or a modern purpose built establishment. Whatever difference there is in the size and character, of these vineyards, they all have one thing in common and that is their delight in seeing visitors.

The history of wine making in England and Wales dates back to Roman times with some of the included vineyards being within the vicinity of these ancient settlements. Mediaeval times saw the next period of wine producing activity, due primarily to the monasteries, and this was then followed by the grand country houses of the 18th century. The present day is the latest period of high activity. It is believed to have been kicked started commercially by Sir Guy Salisbury-Jones in 1952, although there had been some plantings before, at Hambledon vineyard in Hampshire. Not only a village on the wine map but on the cricket map too. Development in the industry has been steady and there are now approximately 800 productive vineyards across the UK. This latest period appears to be connected to what is believed to be climate change where the latent temperatures are getting warmer and therefore more suitable for the ripening of the fruit. New plantings, of vines, appears to grow year on year as more land is deemed to be suitable for this purpose and as existing vineyards develop more of their Estate. Also science has been getting more involved with, amongst other things, the selection of suitable vine clones and root stock.

The vineyards included in this selection vary in size from just a few acres to over 200 acres and are, very often, in areas of the UK renowned for their natural beauty. These vineyards can be small family affairs, where they form part of a much larger agricultural holding, or large exclusive corporate estates. They can also differ in accessibility by either being adjacent to an arterial road or, at the other end of the scale, down some off the beaten track. Similarly they will vary in the range of wines they have on offer. And the visitor goes, hopefully, for the wine and not just the accommodation and the view. The style and character of the resulting wines will depend on the differing choice of grape varieties used, the soils, the orientation and spacing of the planting and the height of the vineyard above sea level. Together with these aspects of the micro-climate, the canopy training and the overall *terroir* influences the ability to be individual. Added to this there are the vagaries of the English climate. Then you have the developing experience of the winemakers, the 'old timers' as well as the newly established who are together now producing world class wines that are being recognised the world over. Their selection of grape varieties, to use in any particular style of wine, and the proportion of each variety, within that style, will produce individuality together with their own distinctive style.

Whilst the book is not intended to be fully comprehensive of all the vineyards that fit into the category of providing overnight accommodation, it does give some indication of what is available, for the visitor, within the vine growing areas of the 'Winelands of England & Wales' under the banner of **English Wine**.

Welcome to the world of **OENOTOURISM**.

Preface

Where a described 'vineyard' is to be found at more than one location it is always the originally planted plot that is detailed within the describing text. This is also most likely the location of any overnight accommodation. Whereas the area 'under vine' is the combined area of all of the plots under the same management and where the 'annual production' is given it is the combined total of bottles produced from all of the plots.

In this book the word 'Classic', in the text description of many of the sparkling wines, is the term recommended by WineGB (Wines of Great Britain) to describe the vinification method of sparkling wines that is the same as that used in the Champagne region of France.

Where a wine is given a 'vintage' (2018) the associated tasting note applies to that specific wine produced from grapes of that particular year. Where a wine is shown as 'non vintage' (NV) the tasting note is for a wine which has a consistency of flavour year on year, by the blending of wines from different years, to produce a distinctive house style for that particular vineyard and that particular wine.

Wines highlighted by the symbol ⭕ have been medal winners in the prestigious annual national and international wine tasting competitions held in this country and abroad.

The photographic illustrations included have all been provided by the vineyards themselves.

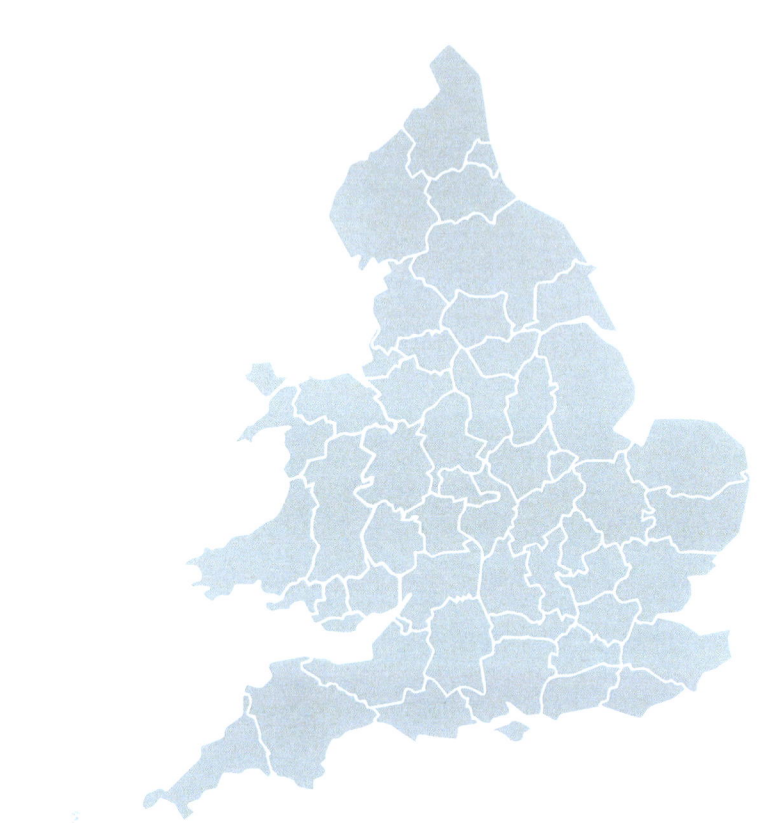

CONTENTS

The South West   12

The South Centre   50

The South East   66

East Anglia and East Midlands   96

West Midlands and South Wales   114

North Wales and North of England   138

THE SOUTH WEST

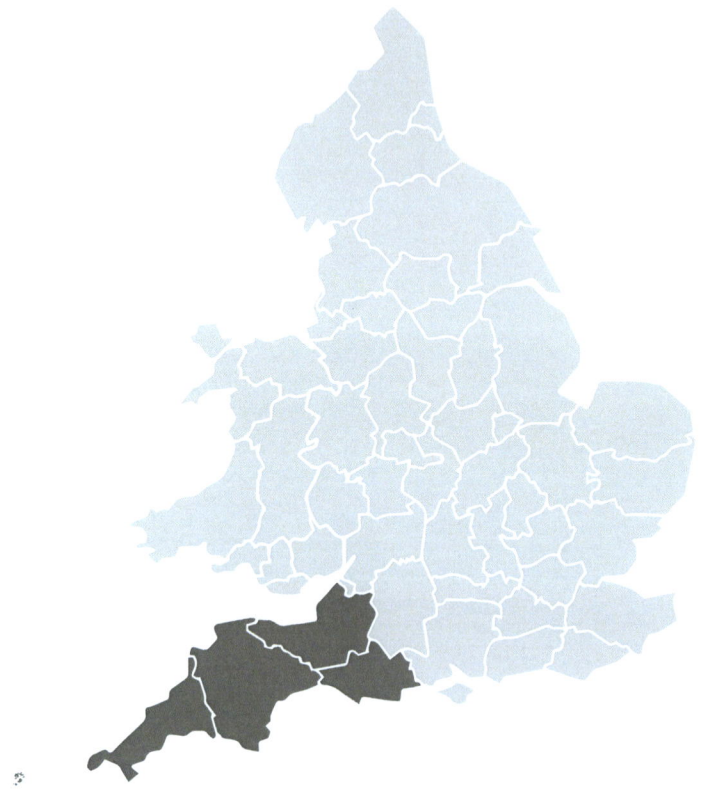

ISLES OF SCILLY

St. Martin's Vineyard   14

CORNWALL

Polgoon Vineyard   16

Trevibban Mill Vineyard (Organic)   20

DEVON

Calancombe Estate Vineyard   24

Castlewood Vineyard   26

Kenton Park Estate Vineyard   28

Old Walls Vineyard   30

Pebblebed Vineyard (Organic)   32

Swanaford Estate Vineyard   34

Ten Acres Vineyard   36

Lympstone Manor   38

DORSET

Melbury Vale Vineyard   40

SOMERSET

Aldwick Estate Vineyard   44

Wraxall Vineyard   46

Secret Valley Vineyard (Organic)   48

ST. MARTIN'S VINEYARD
(Isles of Scilly)

James Faulconbridge & Holly Robbins
Higher Town, St. Martins TR25 0QL
07936 710262
stmartinsvineyard@gmail.com
www.stmartinsvineyard.co.uk

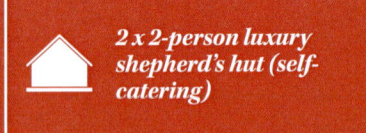

2 x 2-person luxury shepherd's hut (self-catering)

The initial ¾ acre coastal vineyard was planted by Graham & Valerie Thomas on the bulb and cut flower farm belonging to Derek Perkins, Valerie's father, as an experiment to see if it was possible to grow vines successfully on the island. In the same year, as this initial planting, the family had a well dug on the farm to guarantee a constant water supply. Since this early venture was a relative success the vineyard has steadily grown with additional plantings year on year to bring it up to its present size. Due to what can be considered inclement weather, and being so close to the sea, many of the vines are protected in polytunnels as well as by the surrounding hedges. In 2003 an existing stone built barn, on the property, was converted into the vineyard's winery. The vineyard was bought, by the present owners, in 2020 after a casual remark was made, by the previous owners who were looking to retire, during a visitors' tour. They consequently became the owners of what is probably the most southerly self-sufficient vineyard within mainland UK producing 'English Wine' whilst at the same time having a complete change occupation.

Vineyard:
- 2.50 acres under vine
- Around sea level
- Southerly facing slope
- Sandy loam soil on granitic subsoil
- First vines planted in 1996
- Approximately 760 vines to the acre

Winery:
- Still wines – White, Rosé & Red

Cellar Door:
- **Open:**
  Summer months:
  Selected dates
- **Self-guided tour & tasting:**
  Daily when open
- **Self-guided walkabout:**
  When open

Wines: Total wine production of between 1,500 & 3,000 bottles a year
Wine sales at Cellar Door, at selected local stockists & online

Winemakers: James Faulconbridge, Holly Robbins

WHITE

St. Martin's White – 2020
- 11.0% – *Fresh apple/citrus & honeydew melon*
- Orion

St. Martin's Reserve – 2019
- 11.0% – *Passion fruit & lychee/ tropical fruit & apricots*
- Siegerrebe, Reichensteiner

ROSÉ

St. Martin's Rosé – 2020
- 10.0% – *Caramel, toffee & strawberry/cherry & almonds*
- Black Hamburg, Regent

RED

St. Martin's Red – 2020
- 12.0% – *Blackcurrant/fruit flavours & peppery*
- Rondo

POLGOON VINEYARD
(Cornwall)

John & Kim Coulson
Rosé Hill, Penzance TR20 8TE
01736 333946
cheers@polgoon.com   www.polgoon.com

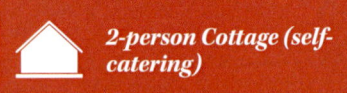

2-person Cottage (self-catering)

On the site of what had been Tomlin Bros Flower Farm, which had been established in the 18th century for growing gladiolis and daffodils, the present owners planted their first 3500 vines on this derelict 21 acres that they had purchased in 2002. This changed their lifestyle completely as they had previously been fish merchants for many years. The existing on site farmhouse, required as space for their growing family, had been built in 1803. They were convinced that in this area just outside Penzance, and one which is subject to maritime influence, they could produce artisan wines as a family operation. This newly planted vineyard is probably the most westerly in mainland UK with views over Mount's Bay towards St. Michael's Mount offshore. Their first vintage, a still rosé, did, however, become a medal winner in more than one open competition. The part of the farm that became the vineyard included an area of polytunnels as well containing many differing varieties of vine including an early planting of Sauvignon Blanc. These polytunnels enable an early, and consistent, ripening of the grapes. The vineyard has, over the years, steadily grown in acreage, and self-containment, with the gradual addition of vines and on-site facilities.

Vineyard:
- *15.00 acres under vine*
- *Around 30m. above sea level*
- *South facing slopes*
- *Well drained sandy loam granitic soil*
- *First vines planted in 2004*
- *Approximately 1,000 vines to the acre*

Winery:
- *Sparkling wines – White & Rosé*
- *Still wines – White, Rosé & Red*

Visitors' Centre:
- **Open:**
  April to December:
  Monday to Saturday (09.00 to 17.00);
  Sunday (10.30 to 16.00)
  January & March:
  Monday to Saturday (09.00 to 17.30)
- **Guided tour & tasting:**
  April to September:
  Wednesday & Thursday (10.30 & 15.00)
- **Self-guided walkabout:**
  When open (11.00 to 15.00).
- **Groups:**
  By prior arrangement only

Wines:

Total wine production of between 25,000 & 35,000 bottles a year
Wine sales at Visitors' Centre, at selected local stockists & online

Winemaker: John Coulson

SPARKLING

Seyval Blanc – 2018
- 12.0% – *Classic Method*
- Brut – *(9.9 g/lt) – Green pear flirt/ citrus & balanced acidity*
- Seyval Blanc *(100%)*

Pinot Noir – 2018
- 12.0% – *Classic Method*
- Brut – *(12.0 g/lt) – Zesty citrus & toasted crumb/tangerine, honey & spice*
- Pinot Noir *(100%)*

WHITE

Seyval Blanc/Ortega – 2018
- 11.0% – *Floral honeysuckle/ butterscotch, white peach & grape*
- Seyval Blanc, Ortega

Ortega – 2017
- % – *Apricot & honeysuckle/peach & stone fruit*
- Ortega

Seyval Blanc – 2021
- 11.0% – *Green grass & grape/juicy citrus & tropical fruit*
- Seyval Blanc

Bacchus – 2021
- 11.5% – *Lime zest & cut grass/ elderflower & gooseberry*
- Bacchus

Sauvignon Blanc – 2021
- 11.5% – *Lime, passion fruit & pineapple/green apple & topical fruit*
- Sauvignon Blanc

ROSÉ

Rondo – 2021
- 11.0% – *Cornish strawberries/red summer berries & crispy acidity*
- Rondo

Pinot Noir Rosé – 2021
- 11.0% – *Summer berries & red cherry/red apple finish*
- Pinot Noir

RED

Rondo – 2021
- 11.0% – *Blackcurrant, redcurrant & plum/smooth vanilla finish*
- Rondo

POLGOON VINEYARD (CORNWALL)

TREVIBBAN MILL VINEYARD (ORGANIC)
(Cornwall)

Engin & Liz Mumcuoglu
Dark Lane, Wadebridge, PL27 7SE
01841 541413
admin@trevibbanmill.com   www.trevibbanmill.com

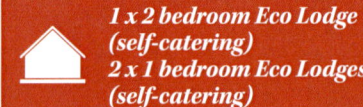

1 x 2 bedroom Eco Lodge (self-catering)
2 x 1 bedroom Eco Lodges (self-catering)

This vineyard is located down a campion lined lane and only a short distance from Padstow, on the north Cornish coast, within the area of the St. Issey Valley. The site was originally bought as a restoration project of the old Miller's residence by the lake. However this original idea developed into something grander. That restoration idea became a development that included a vineyard, a fruit orchard together with open countryside. The old Mill house, dating back to the 18th century and the building that instigated the project, is located within the wooded area adjacent to the pond of the original Mill race. All the new estate buildings take advantage of their orientation by incorporating a large expanse of solar collectors.

Vineyard:
- 7.50 acres under vine
- Between 60 & 90m. above sea level
- South facing slope
- Easy draining poor slatey soil
- First vines planted in 2008
- Approximately 1,400 vines to the acre

Winery:
- Sparkling wines – White & Rosé
- Still wines – White, Rosé & Red

Features:
- Wine Bar
- Function Facilities
- Licensed for civil ceremonies

Visitors' Centre:
- **Open:**
  All year round:
  Wednesday to Sunday (12.00 to 17.00);
  Bank Holidays (12.00 to 17.00)
- **Guided tour & tasting:**
  March to October:
  Wednesday, Thursday & Saturday (16.00)
  By appointment only
- **Groups:**
  By prior arrangement only

Wines: Total wine production of around 30,000 bottles a year
          Wine Sales at Visitors' Centre & online

Winemaker: Engin Mumcuoglu, Salvatore Leone

SPARKLING

Blanc de Blancs – 2015 ◯
- 12.0% – *Classic Method*
- Brut Nature – *(1.5 g/lt) – Lemon yoghurt & fresh apple/notes of toast & marmalade*
- Chardonnay *(100%)*

Black Ewe – 2018 ◯
- 12.0% – *Classic Method*
- Brut – *(1.5 g/lt) – Green apple, lemon & sherbet/fine bubbles*
- Seyval Blanc *(100%)*

Blanc de Noir – 2018
- 12.0% – *Classic Method*
- Brut – *(g/lt) – Ripe peaches, honey & almonds*
- Pinot Noir

Black Ewe Pink– 2020
- 12.0% – *Classic Method*
- Brut – *(7.0 g/lt) – Fresh red berry & cranberry*
- Dornfelder *(100%)*

Pinot Noir Pink – 2015 ◯
- 12.0% – *Classic Method*
- Brut – *(7.0 g/lt) – Strawberries & cream*
- Pinot Noir *(100%)*

WHITE

Black Ewe – 2020 ◯
- 11.5% – *Dry, crisp & zesty/lemon, apple & herbs*
- Pinot Blanc, Ortega

Merope – 2020
- 11.5% – *Fruity, crisp & dry/ gooseberry, kumquat & fruit*
- Seyval Blanc, Reichensteiner, Orion

Harlyn – 2021 ◯
- 11.5% – *Off-dry, aromatic & complex/minerality, stone fruits & honeysuckle*
- Chardonnay, Seyval Blanc, Orion

Constantine – 2020
- 12.0% – *Brown butter, acacia & sweet spice/melon & brioche*
- Chardonnay

ROSÉ

Rock – 2021 ◯
- 11.0% – *Aromatic, dry & complex/ strawberries & cream*
- Dornfelder, Chardonnay

RED

Black Ram – 2018 ◯
- 12.5% – *Dark chocolate & black pepper/black cherry & blackcurrant*
- Dornfelder, Rondo

Black Ewe – 2019 ◯
- 13.0% – *Morello cherries, figs, prunes & vanilla/pepper & tobacco*
- Pinot Noir Precoce

Dark Lane Reserve – 2018
- 14.0% – *Cloves & violets/dried plums & black cherries*
- Dornfelder

TREVIBBAN MILL VINEYARD (ORGANIC) (CORNWALL)

CALANCOMBE ESTATE VINEYARD
(Devon)

Caroline & Lance Whitehead
Nr. Modbury, PL21 0TU
01548 830905
caroline@calancombe-estate.com
www.calancombe-estate.com

1 x 6 bedroom Farmhouse
1 x 1 bedroom holiday Cottage (self-catering)

These present owners bought the 64 acre Estate, in the Witchcombe Valley, in 2011 and proceeded to investigate the possibility of growing vines. The Estate has its origins in the 16th century and is located between Dartmoor and the coast and also borders the Shilston Brook. The area of the Estate selected for the planting of a vineyard was shown to have suitable soils and orientation, as well as its own particular micro-climate. The initial planting was carried out the following year. Over the next few years that initial planting has been steadily extended to bring the vineyard up to its present size. Other facilities, including a recently purpose built modern winery, have been steadily added in time for the initial vintage. These owners have also planted approximately 2.5 acres of blackcurrants and cider apple orchards to add to the many varieties of vine already planted.

Vineyard:
- *23.00 acres under vine*
- *Between 65 & 140m. above sea level*
- *South-west facing slopes*
- *Free draining soils*
- *First vines planted in 2012*
- *Approximately 1,000 vines to the acre*

Winery:
- *Sparkling wine – White*
- *Still wines – White & Rosé*

Distillery:
- *Gins*
- *Cider brandy*

Cider Press:
- *Sparkling cider*
- *Still cider*

Apiary:
- *Honey*
- *Featuring bee keeping experiences*

Visitors' Centre:
- **Open:**
  All year round:
  Thursday to Sunday (11.00 to 17.00)
- **Guided tours & tasting:**
  Twice daily;
  Oher times by appointment only.
- **Private tour & tasting:**
  Any time, by appointment

Wines:
Total wine production of between 30,000 & 40,000 bottles a year
Wine sales at Visitors' Centre, at local & regional stockists & online

Winemakers: Oliver Shaw, Caroline Whitehead

SPARKLING

Blanc de Noirs – 2018
- 12.0% – *Classic Method*
- *Brut – (3.0 g/lt) – Strawberries & citrus/cream, baked apple & gentle spice*
- Pinot Noir *(100%)*

WHITE

Bacchus – 2020
- 10.5% – *Grapefruit & tropical fruit/ gooseberry, citrus & elderflower*
- Bacchus

Vintage Reserve – 2020
- 11.0% – *Fresh & lightly aromatic/ peaches & apricots*
- Madeleine Angevine

White Pinot Noir – 2019
- 10.5% – *Grapefruit, apricot & apple/redcurrant & hantilly*
- Pinot Noir

ROSÉ

Pinot Noir Rosé – 2020
- 10.5% – *Summer fruits & citrus/ peaches & strawberries&cream*
- Pinot Noir

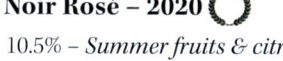

CALANCOMBE ESTATE VINEYARD (DEVON)

CASTLEWOOD VINEYARD
(Devon)

Rob Corbett
Musbury, EX13 8SS
01297 552068
info@castlewoodvineyard.co.uk
www.castlewoodvineyard.co.uk

2 x Grade II listed holiday Cottages (self-catering)

Forming part of an existing much larger family dairy farm this vineyard is situated on the rolling bank side of the River Axe beneath the ancient Hill Fort of Musbury Castle and is planted in unusually wide apart rows. These wide grassed rows reduce shadowing on the vines and also reduce the danger of soil erosion. It also has its own particular micro-climate. The slope also allows any frost to safely roll down the vineyard to the valley floor. The redundant farm buildings have been converted to accommodate the processing equipment required for this self sufficient vineyard. The vineyard initially presses the grapes in small batches using either a basket or bladder press and then follows the traditional method for the sparkling wine. The farm is surrounded by designated areas of outstanding beauty. During the Summer months the vineyard hosts a particular celebratory wine festival.

Vineyard:
- 9.50 acres under vine
- Around 50m. above sea level
- South facing slopes
- Clay loam soils
- First vines planted in 2006
- Approximately 666 vines to the acre

Winery:
- Sparkling wines – White & Rosé
- Still wine – White

Cellar Door:
- **Open:** By appointment only
- **Guided tour & tasting:** By appointment only

Features:
- Function facilities
- Licensed for civil ceremonies

Wines: Total wine production of between 6,000 & 10,000 bottles a year
Wine sales at Cellar Door, at local stockists & online

Winemaker: Rob Corbett

SPARKLING

Brut – NV
- 12.0% – *Classic Method*
- Brut – *(g/lt) – Elderflower & English hedgerow/citrus undertones*
- Chardonnay, Bacchus, Seyval Blanc

Vintage Brut – 2018
- 12.0% – *Classic Method*
- Brut – *(10.2 g/lt) – Elegant & buttery/lemon sherbet & tangerine*
- Pinot Noir *(65%)*, Pinot Meunier *(35%)*

Brut Nature – 2018
- 12.0% – *Classic Method*
- Brut – *(8.0 g/lt) – Elderflower & fresh cut grass/green citrus, ripe lemons & flinty minerality*
- Bacchus *(50%)*, Chardonnay *(50%)*

HIX – 2015
- 12.0% – *Classic Method*
- Brut – *(11.0 g/lt) – Lemon sherbet & honey/creaminess & complexity*
- Chardonnay *(100%)*

Rosé – NV
- 12.0% – *Classic Method*
- Brut – *(10.9 g/lt) – Strawberries&cream/fresh red berries & crisp acidity*
- Pinot Noir, Pinot Meunier

WHITE

Devon Minnow – 2020
- 11.5% – *Citrus fruit & vanilla/ herbal undertones &buttery roundness*
- Bacchus

Artefact – 2020
- 10.18% – *Elderberry, greengage &grapefruit/gentle bitterness*
- Bacchus

CASTLEWOOD VINEYARD (DEVON)

KENTON PARK ESTATE VINEYARD
A member of the **Vineyards of Devon** collective

Matthew Bernstein
Helwell Barton, Kenton, EX6 8NW
01626 682401
kentonparkestate@gmail.com
www.kentonparkestate.com

1 X 2 bedroom holiday cottage (self-catering)
1 x 2 person luxury shepherd's hut (self-catering)

This vineyard is situated within a family farm on the western bank of the River Exe estuary, adjacent to Exeter Racecourse and originally part of the Powderham Castle Estate that was first mentioned in the Doomsday Book of 1086. It was originally planted as Kenton Vineyard however when these new, and present, owners bought it in 2017 they renamed it, as the Park Estate, and then completely replanted the vineyard in 2018. Its location on the foothills of Haldon Forest, and overlooked by the ridge of Mamhead Forest, enables it to enjoy a particular micro-climate beneficial to the growing of grapes. The vineyard forms just one feature within this family owned Country Sporting Estate which has many adventure experiences including the free range rare breed sheep, that are part of a breeding programme, the pygmy goats and other roaming ducks and chickens.

Vineyard:
- *20.00 acres under vine*
- *Around m. above sea level*
- *South facing slopes*
- *Sandy soils*
- *First vines planted in 2003*
- *Approximately vines to the acre*

Winery:
- *Sparkling wines – White & Rosé*
- *Still wine – White & Rosé*

Distillery:
- *Gin*

Brewery:
- *Craft ales*

Cider Press:
- *Sparkling cider*

Visitors' Centre:
- **Open:**
  All year round:
  Tuesday to Thursday & Saturday (10.00 to 16.00);
  Friday (18.00 to 23.30)
- **Guided tour & tastings:**
  By appointment only

Features:
- *Vineyard experiences*
- *Café/Restaurant*
- *Function facilities*

Wines: Total wine production of around bottles a year
Wine sales at Visitors' Centre & online

Winemaker: Ben Oliphant-Thompson

SPARKLING

Classic Cuvée – NV
- 12.0% – *Classic Method*
- Brut – *(g/lt) – Brioche, toast & rip stone fruit/citrus fruit*
- Chardonnay, Pinot Noir, Pinot Meunier

Flying Circus –
- 12.0% – *Classic Method*
- Brut – *(g/lt) – Stone & citrus fruit/ lemon & orchard apples*
- Chardonnay

Gun Dog Escape – 2014
- 11.5% – *Classic Method*
- Brut – *(g/lt) – Summer fruits & fresh fruity berries/hints of vanilla*
- Pinot Noir *(90%)*, Pinot Meunier *(10%)*

Rosé –2020
- 11.5% – *Charmat Method*
- *Summer fruits & berries/citrus & floral notes*
- Pinot Noir, Reichensteiner

WHITE

Grape Escape – 2021
- 11.5% – *Fresh elderflower & pear/ English hedgerow & summer flavours*
- Bacchus, Reichensteiner

ROSE

Pigeage Rosé – 2021
- 13.0% – *Wild strawberries, raspberries/floral notes*
- Solaris, Pinotin

KENTON PARK ESTATE VINEYARD (DEVON)

OLD WALLS VINEYARD
A member of the **Vineyards of Devon** collective

Michael Smyth
Old Walls Road, Bishopsteignton
TQ14 9PQ   01626 770877
enquiries@oldwallsvineyard.co.uk
www.oldwallsvineyard.co.uk

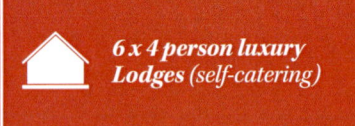

6 x 4 person luxury Lodges (self-catering)

Ken and Lesley Dawe's family had farmed the land for over 90 years when they decided to plant a vineyard to supplement their income. They created their vineyard on an area of land, on the northern bankside of the River Teign, and just a short distance inland from the coast, that it is believed had been used as a vineyard in Roman times. There is also evidence of Medieval occupancy. In 1258 Walter Bronsecombe became Bishop of Exeter and commenced to build himself Bishop's Palace. Parts of this early building still remain on the site and it is from these ruins that the vineyard takes its name. They have continually developed and diversified the vineyard over the years for it to become and contain what it does today.

Vineyard:
- 7.50 acres under vine
- Around m. above sea level
- South facing slope
- Red Devon sandstone soils
- First vines planted in 2002
- Approximately 1,000 vines to the acre

Winery:
- Sparkling wines – White & Rosé
- Still wines – White, Rosé & Red

Cellar Door:
- **Open:**
  All year round:
  Sunday to Thursday (09.30 to 16.30);
  Friday & Saturday (09.30 to 23.00)
- **Guided tour & tasting:**
  April to September:
  Weekly – Friday & Saturday (15.00);
  Monthly – 1st & 3rd Sunday (15.00)
  October to March:
  Friday, Saturday & Sunday (14.00)

Features:
- Café/Restaurant
- Function facilities

Wines:
Total wine production of around 26,000 bottles a year
Wine sales at Cellar Door & online

Winemaker: Hans Schliefer

SPARKLING

White – 2014
( )% – *Classic Method*
Brut – *(g/lt) –*
Auxerrois *(%),* Pinot Noir Precoce *(%)*

Rosé – 2014
( )% – *Classic Method*
Brut – *(g/lt) –*
Pinot Noir Precoce *(%),* Auxerrrois *(%)*

WHITE

Bacchus – NV
( )% –
Bacchus

Priory Dry – NV
( )% –
Reichensteiner

Chapel Medium – NV
( )% –
Reichensteiner

ROSÉ

Rosé – NV
( )% –
Pinot Noir

Bishops Blush – NV
( )% –
Rondo

Bishops Blush Medium – NV
( )% –
Rondo

RED

Palace Red – NV
( )% – *Palatable/blackberry overtones & good length*
Regent, Rondo, Dunkelfelder

Palace Red Reserve – NV
( )% –
Rondo, Regent, Dunkelfelder

OLD WALLS VINEYARD (DEVON)

PEBBLEBED VINEYARD (ORGANIC)
(Devon)

Anna Bowen
Marianne Pool Farm, Ebford Lane,
Clyst St. George, EX3 0NZ
01392 875908
www.pebblebed.co.uk

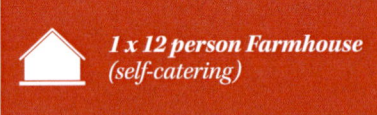
1 x 12 person Farmhouse (self-catering)

When Geoff Bowen, a hydrogeologist by profession, found a suitable ½ acre plot of land, at a friend's house in 1999, he and 10 other families formed a co-operative and planted some vines. This became Ebford Vineyard. This single planting has grown into a vineyard spread over four sites under Geoff's management. Each site has its own soil and planted grape varieties and thus give the winemaker plenty of scope for the style and composition of the final wines. The original site, close to the River Exe, now houses the vineyard's winery and Cellar Door. The resulting still wine was an early user of the screw top bottle. In 2010 Geoff appeared on the TV programme 'The Dragon's Den' where he enlisted the support of Duncan Bannatyne to continue his social programme. Unfortunately Geoff has recently died before seeing the various sites reach their full potential. The vineyard, now managed by Geoff's widow, also has a sales outlet at its Wine Bar on the banks of the River Exe at Topsham (EX3 0JJ).

Vineyard:
- 20.00 acres under vine
- Around m. above sea level
- South facing gentle slope
- Sandy loam soil with underlying sand, marl & pebblebeds
- First vines planted in 2002
- Approximately vines to the acre

Winery:
- Sparkling wine – White
- Still wines – White, Rosé & Red

Cellar Door:
- **Open:**
  May to September:
  Thursday to Saturday (11.00 to 15.00)
  By appointment only
- **Guided tour & tasting**
  Thursday (16.00) &
  Saturday (11.00 & 15.00)
  By appointment only
- **Groups:**
  By prior arrangement only

Wines:
Total wine production of around 50,000 bottles a year
Wine sales at Cellar Door, at local stockists & online

Winemaker: Alex Mills

SPARKLING

Sparkling White – NV
- 11.5% - *Classic method*
- Brut - (g/lt) - *Crisp green apple/ lime, buttery brioche & citrus notes*
- Seyval Blanc

Sparkling Rosé – NV
- 11.5% - *Classic method*
- Brut - (g/lt) – *Delicate red berry & rosé petal flavours/fresh acidity*
- Seyval Blanc, Rondo

WHITE

White – NV
- 10.0% – *Lime & elderflower/ tropical fruits, grapefruit, lychee & minerally finish*
- Madeleine Angevine, Phoenix, Seyval Blanc

ROSÉ

Rosé – NV
- 10.0% – *Cherry & redcurrant/ caramel & crisp acidity*
- Seyval Blanc, Rondo

RED

Red – NV
- 11.0% – *Spice & herbal hints/ cherry, plum & chocolatey finish*
- Rondo, Regent, Pinot Noir

PEBBLEBED VINEYARD (ORGANIC) (DEVON)

SWANAFORD ESTATE VINEYARD
A member of the **Vineyards of Devon** collective

Ben & Caroline Goulden
Swanaford Road, Bridford, EX6 7HG
01647 252846
ben@swanaford.com
www.swanaford.com

2 x 1 bedroom holiday Cottages (self-catering)
1 x 2 bedroom holiday Cottage (self-catering)

This family-run vineyard has been planted on the south-eastern facing bank of the River Teign. It forms a small part of the 50-acre Estate bought by the family in 2012 on their move from London. Having spent time preparing the land, all 10,000 vines were planted at one go in one day the following year. A recent development has been the building of the Visitors' Centre in 2017, and the vineyard continues to develop its facilities and offerings.

Vineyard:
- 10.00 acres under vine
- Around 60m. above sea level
- South eastern facing slopes
- Sandy loam soil
- First vines planted in 2013
- Approximately 1,000 vines to the acre

Winery:
- Sparkling wines – White & Rosé
- Still wine – White

Visitors' Centre:
- **Open:**
  Easter to September;
  Other times
  By appointment only
- **Guided tour & tasting:**
  Sunday (11.30);
  Occasional Friday (17.30)

Wines: Wine sales at the Visitors' Centre, at selected local stockists & online

Winemaker: Ben Goulden

SPARKLING

Classic Cuvée – 2018
- 12.0% – *Classic Method*
- Brut – *(9.0 g/lt) – Floral/brioche notes, zesty apple & citrus fruit*
- Chardonnay *(60%)*, Pinot Noir *(30%)*, Pinot Meunier *(10%)*

Rosé – 2018 ○
- 12.0% – *Classic Method*
- Brut – *(10.0 g/lt) – Summer berry flavours/citrus notes & fine mousse*
- Chardonnay *(50 %)*, Pinot Noir *(35 %)*, Pinot Meunier *(15 %)*

WHITE

Estate White – NV
- 11.0% – *Aromatic & dry/hints of lychee, passion fruit & peaches*
- Siegerrebe, Schonburger

Kingfisher – NV
- 11.0% – *Aromatic/tropical fruit flavours*
- Bacchus

SWANAFORD ESTATE VINEYARD (DEVON)

TEN ACRES VINEYARD
A member of the **Vineyards of Devon** collective

Toby & Esther McKinnel
Ten Acres, Winkleigh, EX19 8EY
01837 83892
tenacrescamping@hotmail.co.uk
www.tenacresvineyardcamping.co.uk

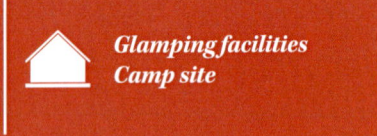

Glamping facilities
Camp site

The vineyard can be found down a quiet county tack, away from traffic, and on the edge of what used to be Winkleigh's wartime airfield. This is on the edge of Dartmoor, which can be seen from the vineyard, and whose openness has a considerable influence on the weather encountered at the vineyard. The wines from this vineyard are primarily for the visitors to the camping facilities as this is the owners' principal sales outlet. These owners moved to the area in 2007 after having spent the previous five years living in Hungary where they enjoyed a similar lifestyle.

Vineyard:
- 2.50 acres under vine
- Around 150m. above sea level
- South facing slope
- Loam soil over Schist slate
- First vines planted in 2008
- Approximately 1,000 vines to the acre

Winery:
- Sparkling wine – White
- Still wine – White

Features:
- Camp shop
- Fruit Press sales

Vineyard Shop:
- **Open:**
  May to September:
  Sunday to Tuesday,
  Thursday to Saturday (10.00 to 20.00);
  Other times by appointment only
- **Guided tour & tasting:**
  Every Saturday (16.30)
  By appointment only
- **Self-guided walkabout:**
  When open
- **Private groups by prior arrangement only:**
  Min. 6 people

Wines: Total wine production of between 2,000 & 10,000 bottles a year
Wine sales at Vineyard Shop, at farmers' markets & online

Winemaker: Toby McKinnel

SPARKLING

Wild Goose – 20120
- 12.0% – *Classic Method*
- Extra Brut – *(6.0 g/lt) – Fruity/soft acidity*
- Madeleine Angevine *(100%)*

Skylark – 2019
- 12.0% – *Classic Method*
- Brut – *(10.0 g/lt) – Tropical fruit*
- Zalagyongye *(80%)*, Seyval Blanc *(20%)*

Rosefinch – 2019
- 12.0% – *Classic Method*
- Brut – *(12.0 g/lt) – Summer fruit flavours*
- Rondo (1/3), Zalagyongye (1/3), Seyval Blanc (1/3)

White Buzzard – 2018
- 12.0% – *Classic Method*
- Brut – *(g/lt) – Gooseberry nose/melon notes*
- Seyval Blanc

WHITE

Greenfinch – 2020
- 11.0% – *Grapefruit & Lime notes*
- Zalagyongye

TEN ACRES VINEYARD (DEVON)

LYMPSTONE MANOR
A Member of the Relais et Chateaux Group

Alex McEwen
Courtlands Lane, Exmouth, EX8 3NZ
01395 202040
welcome@lympstonemanor.co.uk
www.lympstonemanor.co.uk

21 en-suite Luxury Bedrooms (Bed & Breakfast)
5 x 2/5 person Luxury Shepherd's Huts (Bed & Breakfast)

When purchasing this dilapidated Grade II listed Georgian mansion in 2014 the Chef Michael Caines, M.B.E. intended to create a vineyard, together with a welcome stay, that was capable of producing top class sparkling wines. He opened the restored and extended building as an hotel in 2017. This resulting hotel is located within a 23 acre remnant of what had been a 70 acre 1760's Estate created by the Baring banking family and known as Courtland House. The Estate has had many family members as occupants. One created W.H.Smith, the stationers, and another was Princess Diana's great grandmother. All these occupants have made many changes to the house and grounds during their tenure. The Estate, siting on the eastern bank of the River Exe, slopes gently down to the mud flats of the river estuary and comprises of areas of woodland and ancient ponds together with many pieces of original sculpture and the vineyard. It is considered to be a 'Site of Special Scientific Interest'. The vineyard itself benefits from a particular micro climate which together with the local soils provides a first class terroir for growing grapes. Indeed it is considered to be one of the finest in the UK.

Vineyard:
- 11.0 acres under vine
- Around ...m. above sea level
- South westerly aspect
- Red Devon soil over clay
- First vines planted in 2018
- Approximately 1,600 vines to the acre

- Sparkling wine - White
- Still wine - White, Rosé & Red

Open:
- *All year round to hotel residents:*
- **Guided tour & tasting:**
  (hotel residents)
- **Guided tour & tasting with lunch:**
  May to September:
  Wednesday (10.45)

Features:
- Michelin star Restaurant
- Function facilities
- Licensed for civil Ceremonies

Wines: Total wine production of around ... bottles a year.
Wine sales to residents

Winemaker: Liam Idzikowski (at Lyme Bay winery)

SPARKLING

Cuvée - 2020
- (%) – *Classic Method*
- Brut – *(g/lt) -*
- Chardonnay (%), Pinot Noir (%), Pinot Meunier (%)

WHITE

White
- (%) -
- Chardonnay

ROSE

Isabeau - 2022
- (%) -
- Pinot Noir

RED

Triassic Park - 2020
- *(%) – Cherry blossom & rosé aromas/pink apple, strawberry & red plum skins*
- Pinot Noir

MELBURY VALE VINEYARD
(Dorset)

Clare Pestell
Foots Hill, Cann, Shaftesbury, SP7 0BW
01747 854206
info@mvwinery.co.uk
www.mvwinery.co.uk

1 x 2 bedroom Cottage (self-catering)
3 x large Barrels (Glamping/self-catering)

Situated on Foots Hill, in the rolling Dorset countryside, this brother and sister bought 28 acres of derelict and delapidated farmland and buildings, that had been part of Barfoot Farm, in 2003. Their intention was to restore and convert these existing the lands and buildings. However they found an area, after proper investigation, that was suitable for vines and consequently planted their vineyard in 2006. This was on the hillside in the Stirkel Valley at Cann Bridge. The purpose built winery, which is built into the hillside and contains many sustainable features, followed in 2013. These features include a flower meadow on the roof and a rainwater harvesting system. A co-operative has now been formed with many of the small newly planted vineyards in this part of Dorset based around this winery. Another feature associated with the vineyard is a Christmas tree plantation.

Vineyard:
- *2.00 acres under vine*
- *Around 150m. above sea level*
- *South facing slopes*
- *Clay & Greensand soils*
- *First vines planted in 2006*
- *Approximately 1,000 vines to the acre*

Winery:
- *Sparkling wines – White & Rosé*
- *Still wines – White, Rosé & Red*

Distillery:
- *Brandy*

Cider Press:
- *Still cider*

Cellar Door:
- **Open:**
  February to December:
  Friday & Saturday (10.00 to 16.00)
  December:
  Sunday (10.00 to 14.00)
- **Guided tour, tasting & local produce lunch:**
  February to September:
  Friday & Saturday (10.30)
- **Private groups & events:**
  By prior arrangement only
  Min. 10 people

Wines: Total wine production of around 15,000 bottles a year
Wine sales at Cellar Door, at selected local stockists & online

Winemaker: Clare Pestell

SPARKLING

Grace – NV
- 12.0% – *Classic Method*
- Brut – *(11.0 g/lt) – Fresh citrus & ripe pear/green apple, elderflower & meyer lemon*
- Seyval Blanc, Reichensteiner

Decadence Rosé – NV
- 12.5% – *Classic Method*
- Brut – *(12.5 g/lt) – Fresh summer berries & meadow flowers/ strawberry, watermelon & lime zest*
- Seyval Blanc *(95%)*, Pinot Noir *(5%)*

WHITE

Elegance – NV
- 10.5% – *Bright grapefruit & elderflower/white peach & fresh herbs*
- Bacchus

ROSÉ

Virtue – NV
- 11.0% – *Strawberry/bright red summer berries*
- Dornfelder, Reichensteiner

RED

Exuberance – NV
- 10.0% – *Dry & fruity/notes of spice*
- Triomphe, Dornfelder, Rondo, Pinot Noir

The Signature – Batch 02
- 11.5% – *wild cherry, fig & bramble/ cranberry, pomegranate & hibiscus*
- Red & Rosé blend

MELBURY VALE VINEYARD (DORSET)

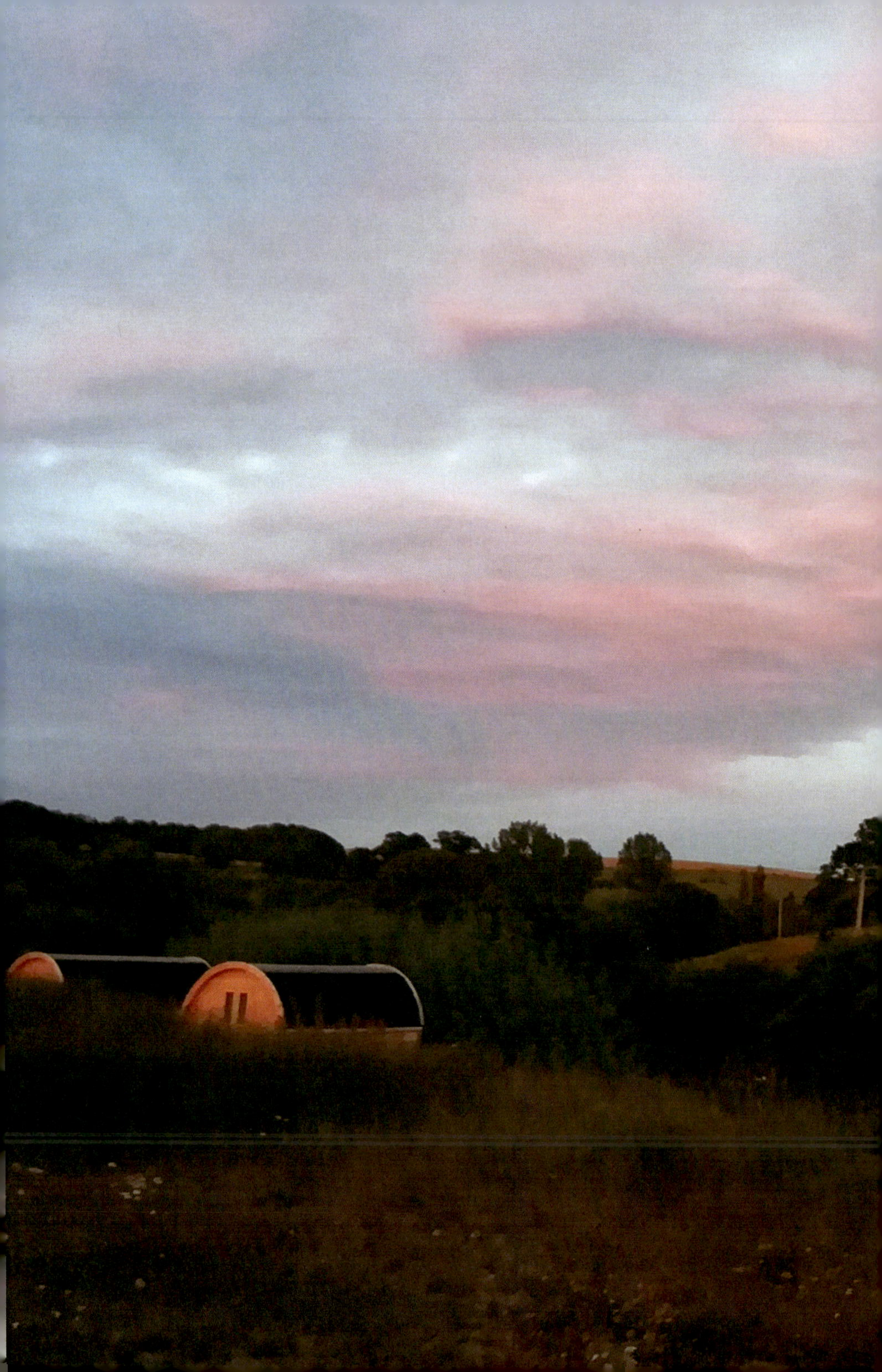

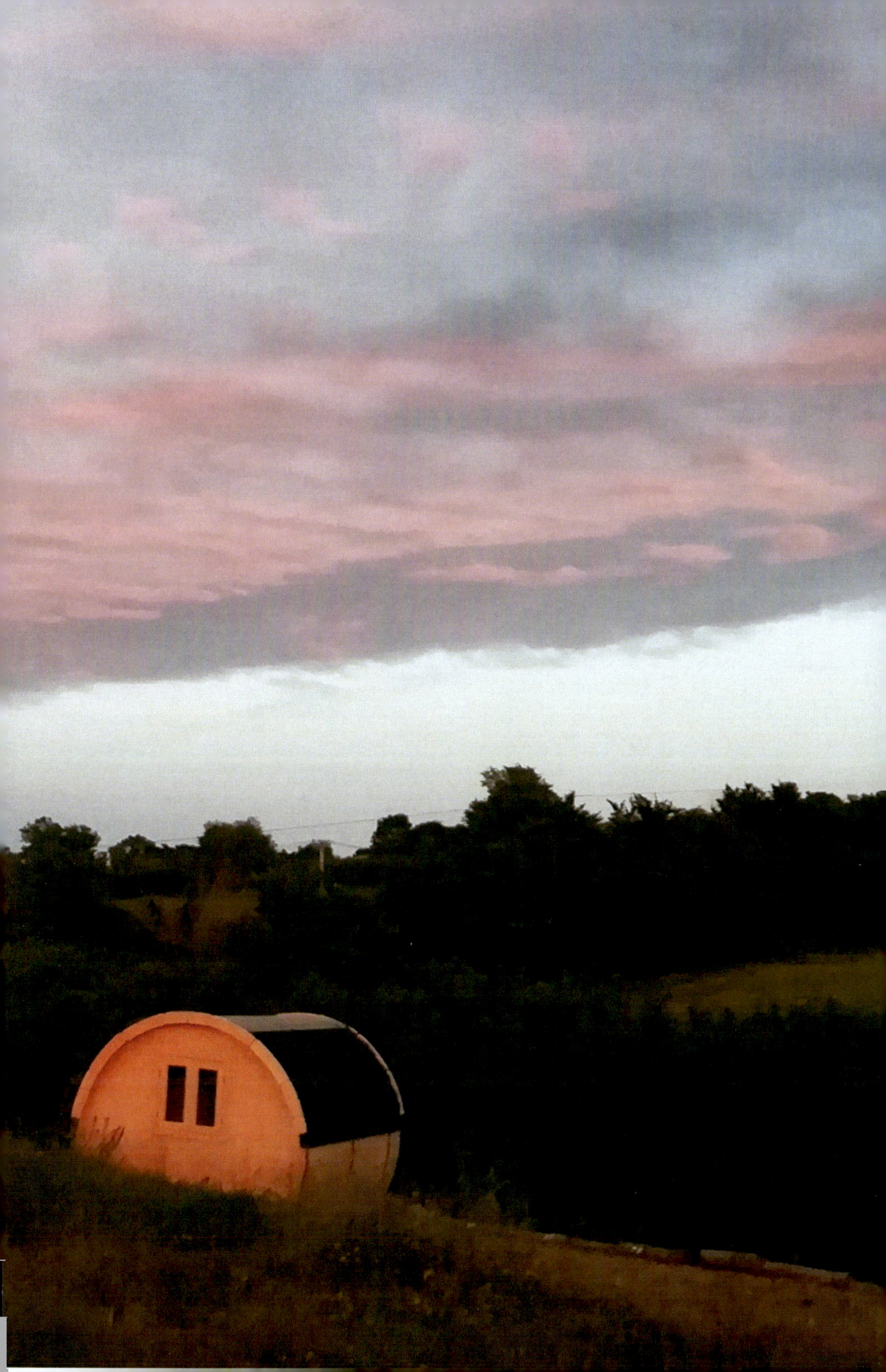

ALDWICK ESTATE VINEYARD
(Somerset)

Carole & Howard Watts
Aldwick Court Farm, Redhill, Blagdon,
BS40 5RS   01934 864404
vineyard@aldwickcourtfarm.co.uk
www.aldwickestate.co.uk

4 en-suite bedrooms (bed & breakfast)
1 x 1 bedroom Apartment (self-catering)

Sitting in the heart of the Yeo Valley, called 'Mercrigge' by the Saxons and 'Alduic' in the Doomsday Book, the vineyard has been planted adjacent to the Mendip Hills Area of Outstanding Natural Beauty is the Dibble 300 acre family farm which they have occupied since 1905. It is now managed and run by the fourth generation of the family with the third generation being the planters of the vineyard. The first planting, to create the vineyard, was by Chris Watts the present owner's brother and was of 2.2 acres. It was followed by the remaining acreage two years later. Some moderate replanting has taken place since those early days to give a more consistant supply of grapes. Since 2009 the existing farm buildings have gradually been remodelled and renovated to provide the facilities for the vineyard and to give this area of the farm its new lease of life. The vineyard has been awarded 'Drinks Producer of the Year – 2019' by the *Western Daily Press*.

Vineyard:
- 11.00 acres under vine
- Around 38m. above sea level
- South and south-westerly aspects
- Clay soil over limestone
- First vines planted in 2008
- Approximately 1,000 vines to the acre

- Sparkling wine – Rosé
- Still wines – White, Rosé & Red

Features:
- Restaurant
- Function facilities
- Licensed for civil ceremonies

Cellar Door:
- **Open:**
  All year round:
  Monday to Thursday (10.00 to 17.00);
  Friday, Weekends & Bank Holidays
  By appointment only
- **Guided tour & tasting:**
  May to October:
  Wednesday (12.00 & 14.30)
  Sunday (12.00 & 14.30)
  By appointment only
- **Groups**:
  By prior arrangement only

Wines:
Total wine production of around 26,000 bottles a year
Wine sales at Cellar Door & online

Winemaker:
Steve Brooksbank (at Bagborough Winery)

SPARKLING

Jubilate Rosé – 2022
- 11.5% – *Classic Method*
- Brut – *(6.7 g/lt) – Delicate, dry & floral/cherries & red fruit*
- Pinot Noir *(100%)*

WHITE

BS40 – 2022
- 11.5% – *Tropical fruit*
- Seyval Blanc, Madeleine Angevine, Solaris

Bacchus – 2021
- 11.5% – *Elderflower, citrus peel & green apple/ herbaceous notes*
- Bacchus

ROSÉ

Mary's Rosé – 2019
- 12.0% – *Aromatic & dry/lychee, pineapple & pear*
- Pinot Noir, Regent, Solaris

RED

Flying Pig – 2022
- 10.5% – *Light to medium bodied/ cinnamon & hint of black cherries*
- Regent, Pinot Noir

ALDWICK ESTATE VINEYARD (SOMERSET)

WRAXALL VINEYARD
(Somerset)

David Bailey & Lexa Hunt,
Wraxall, Shepton Mallet, BA4 6AQ
07508 051209
info@wraxallvineyard.co.uk
www.wraxallvineyard.co.uk

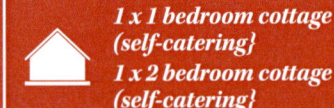

1 x 1 bedroom cottage
(self-catering)
1 x 2 bedroom cottage
(self-catering)

This is a vineyard with a chequered history. In the early 1970s the owners of Wraxall Lodge thought that the field adjacent to their house might be suitable for a vineyard. The resulting planting is situated to the south of the Mendip Hills and has views of the Somerset Levels and with the Dorset Hills in the distance. It is protected by banks of mature trees and with its particular soils and micro-climate appears to have a near perfect terroir. In the 1980's it was bought by the Wagnerian operatic singer Raimund Herincx and his wife Astra Blair. During their ownership its wines were served at the Waldorf Hotel, in London, and other prestige locations. After these owners sold the vineyard it suffered a period of decline but was then rescued by Jackie Brayton who bought it in 2007. The vineyard then began an era of rejuvenation which these present owners, who bought it in 2021 with the intention of making it their family home, intend to continue. They envisage more planting and other improvements. The existing winery building, which dates back to 1876, has been converted into holiday accommodation with a new winery and Visitors' Centre being built.

Vineyard:
- 6.00 acres under vine
- Between 58 & 98m. above sea level
- South facing slope
- Sandy silt loam soil over silty clay
- First vines planted in 1974
- Approximately ... vines to the acre

Winery:
- Sparkling wine - white
- Still wines - white & Rosé

Cellar Door:
- **Open:**
  All year round:
  Monday to Friday (11.00 to 16.00)
  Other times: (contact vineyard first)
  May to September:
- **Guided tour & tasting:**
  Friday (14.00)
  By appointment only
- **Groups:**
  By prior arrangement only

Wines: Total wine production of ... bottles a year
Wine sales at the Cellar Door & online

SPARKLING

Sparkling White - 2018
- 12.0% – *Classic Method*
- Brut – *(g/lt) - Baked apple/gentle fruit flavours & soft mousse*

(%)

WHITE

Bacchus - 2021
- 12.5% – *Aromatic nose/fleshy stone fruits & grapefruit zest*
- Bacchus

ROSÉ

Early Pinot Noir Rosé - NV
- 12.0% – *Crushed raspberry & floral notes/red berry fruits*
- Pinot Noir Precoce

WRAXALL VINEYARD (SOMERSET)

SECRET VALLEY VINEYARD (ORGANIC)
(Somerset)

John & Jan Hardwick
Cobbs Cross Farm, Goathurst, TA5 2DN
01278 671945
enquiries@secret-valley.co.uk
www.secret-valley.co.uk

32 various style units (self-catering/Glamping facilities)

This vineyard, which forms a fairly recent addition, forms one element of a multi-faceted agricultural Estate that contains many different elements. It is situated on the southernmost area of the Quantock Hills Area of Outstanding Natural Beauty. The Estate has been in the same family's ownership since 1973 and is now very much a family affair with all the family members employed in its various activities. As part of its sustainable development it became organic in 2000. Other elements within this well wooded, as well as open, Estate are its main income from Christmas trees together with it being a centre for Outdoor Activities. There are also a number of select breed animals wandering around.

Vineyard:
- *6.00 acres under vine*
- *Around 150m. above sea level*
- *South westerly slope*
- *Sandy loam soils*
- *First vines planted in 2008*
- *Approximately 4,000 vines to the acre*

- *Sparkling wine – White*
- *Still wines – White, Rosé & Red*

Features:
- *Recreational facilities*
- *Outdoor pursuits Centre*
- *Function facilities*
- *Licenced for civil ceremonies*

Cellar Door:
- **Open:**
  March to October:
- **Tour & tasting:**
  By appointment only
- **Self-guided walkabout:**
  When open

Wines: Total wine production of around 3,000 to 4,000 bottles a year
Wine sales at Cellar Door & online

Winemaker: Martin Fowke (at Three Choirs vineyard)

SPARKLING

Sparkling White - 2018
- ()% – *Classic Method*
- Brut – *(g/lt) - Brut - (g/lt) - Citrus notes/green apple flavours & subtle sweetness*
- Pinot Noir, Orion

WHITE

White – 2018
- 11.0% – *Hedgerow aromas/crisp apple, elderflower & cut grass*
- Solaris, Orion, Seyval Blanc

ROSÉ

Rosé – 2018
- 11.5% – *Strawberry & raspberry/ summer fruits & hedgerow*
- Orion, Solaris, Rondo

RED

Red – 2018
- 11.5% – *Blackberry & cherry/ damson, cherry & light pepper*
- Pinot Noir Precoce, Rondo

SECRET VALLEY VINEYARD (ORGANIC) (SOMERSET)

THE SOUTH CENTRE

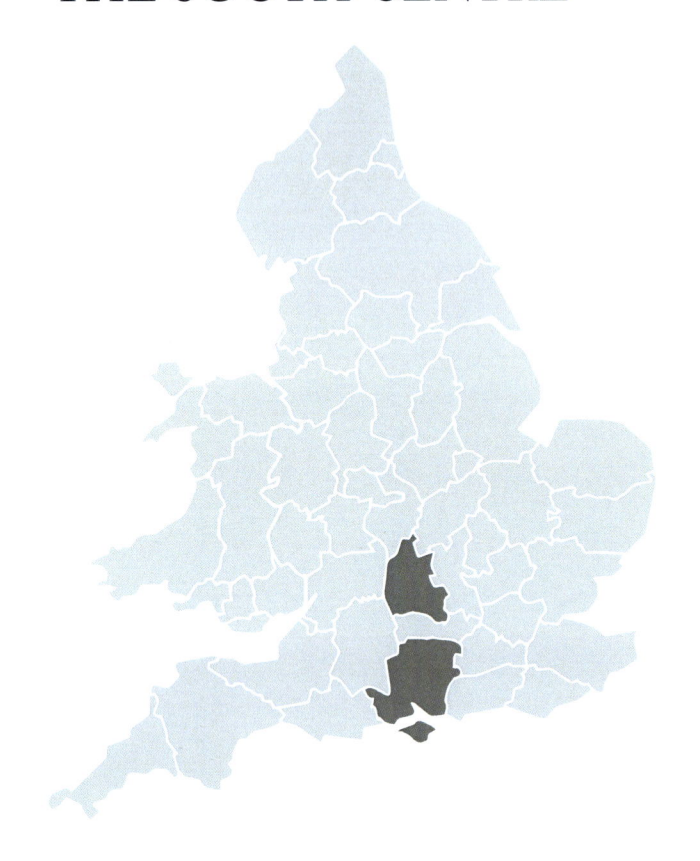

ISLE OF WIGHT

Adgestone Vineyard   52

HAMPSHIRE

Black Chalk Wine   54

Setley Ridge Vineyard   56

OXFORDSHIRE

Brightwell Vineyard   58

Chiltern Valley Vineyard   62

ADGESTONE VINEYARD
(Isle of Wight)

Russell & Philippa Broughton
Upper Road, Brading, PO36 0ES
01983 402882
bookings@adgestonevineyard.co.uk
www.adgestonevineyard.co.uk

1 x 2 person Studio (self-catering)
1 x 2 person Shepherd's Hut (self-catering)

When Ken Barlow established this vineyard on the slopes of Brading Down in 1968 it was to be the first on the island, in modern times, and became one of the early new generation of vineyards in the UK. It was on the site of what may have been a Roman vineyard as it is near to the site of a Roman villa that had belonged to someone of high rank. He had spent 20 years in agricultural research and recognised that the micro-climate on the island, together with the soils, would probably be advantageous for growing vines. With its own underground cellars, one of only a few UK vineyards, and together with its own winery it formed a completely self-contained vineyard. These present owners came to the vineyard in 2013 when they bought it, in a fairly run down state, from Alan and Gill Stockman who had originally bought it in 1995. They then carried out extensive modernisation and replanting to bring the vineyard up to its present state.

Vineyard:
- 10.00 acres under vine
- Between 45 & 60m. above sea level
- South facing slopes
- Chalky loam soils
- First vines planted in 1968
- Approximately 1,150 vines to the acre

Winery:
- Sparkling wines – White & Blue
- Still wines – White, Rosé & Red

Vineyard Shop:
- **Open:**
  All year round:
  Wednesday to Saturday
  (10.00 to 16.00);
  Sunday (11.00 to 16.00)
- **Audio tour & tutored tasting:**
  When open
- **Self-guided walkabout:**
  When open
- **Groups**
  By prior arrangement only

Features:
- Bistro
- Musical events

Wines: Total wine production of around 22,000 bottles a year
Wine sales at Vineyard Shop & online

Winemaker: Russell Broughton

SPARKLING

Classic Cuvée – NV
- 12.5% – *Classic Method*
- Brut – *(0.0 g/lt) – Dry & fruity*
- Orion *(100%)*

Something Blue – NV
- 12.5% – *Classic Method*
- Brut – *(0.0 g/lt) – Fruity*
- Phoenix *(50%)*, Seyval Blanc *(30%)*, Orion *(20%)*, Rondo skin

WHITE

Dry Wight – 2018
- 11.5% – *Crisp & light/fresh green apple & citrus*
- Seyval Blanc, Phoenix

Oaked Wight – 2018
- 11.5% – *Soft & buttery*
- Phoenix, Seyval Blanc

ROSÉ

Blush – 2018
- 11.5% – *Fresh rosé & ripe fruit aromas/soft citrus notes*
- Schonburger, Pinot Noir

RED

Full Bodied Red – 2018 ()
- 12.5% – *Rich blackberry & caramel/fruit & smoked oak*
- Rondo, Regent

BLACK CHALK WINE
A member of the **Vineyards of Hampshire** Group

Jacob Leadley
The Old Dairy, Fullerton Road, Andover,
SP11 7JX
01264 860440
info@blackchalkwine.co.uk
www.blackchalkwine.co.uk

4 x 2 person luxury Tree Houses (self-catering) Under separate ownership

This vineyard was initially planted by Hugh Liddell on parts of the family's 1,200 acre Fullerton Estate in 2005. His original still wine was produced off-site. The vineyard was enlarged by further plantings in 2007, 2008 and 2011. These later plantings allowed a change of direction from the production of a still wine to the concentration on sparkling wines that were still made off-site. Situated on the banks of the River Test the vineyard benefits from its own micro-climate. One particular planting is in a circular formation giving a large gathering area at its centre. This present owner took over the management of the vineyard in 2019 and commenced the development of the site so that all the elements and features of the wine making process can be found in one location.

Vineyard:

- 30.00 acres under vine
- Between 40 & 70m. above sea level
- South-east to south-west facing slopes
- Chalky soils
- First vines planted in 2005
- Approximately 1,700 vines to the acre

Winery:

- Sparkling wines – White & Rosé
- Still wine – Rosé

Tasting Room & Shop:

- **Open:**
  All year round
- **Guided tour & tasting:**
  Friday, Saturday & Sunday (13.30)
- **Guided tour, tasting & lunch:**
  Thursday to Sunday (11.00)
- **Treehouse tasting:**
  Monday, Thursday, Friday & Sunday
  By appointment only

Features:

- Function facilities

Wines: Total wine production of around 35,000 bottles a year
Wine sales at Tasting Room and Shop, at selected local & national stockists & online

Winemakers: Jacob Leadley, Zoe Driver

SPARKLING

Classic – 2018 ◯
- ( )% – *Classic Method*
- Brut – *(g/lt) – Fruit driven complexity/crispy balance*
- Chardonnay *(45%)*, Pinot Meunier *(32%)*, Pinot Noir *(23%)*

Wild Rosé – 2018
- ( )% – *Classic Method*
- Brut – *(g/lt) – Rich, pure raspberries & strawberries/good complexity & clean, crisp finish*
- Pinot Meunier *(51%)*, Pinot Noir *(33%)*, Chardonnay *(16%)*

ROSÉ

Dancer in Pink – 2021
- ( )% – *Ripe strawberries & cherry blossom/red fruits & hints of peach*
- Pinot Noir, Pinot Noir Precoce, Pinot Gris

BLACK CHALK WINE (HAMPSHIRE)

SETLEY RIDGE VINEYARD
A supporter of The New Forest Marque (Hampshire)

Paul & Hayley Girling
Lymington Road, Brockenhurst
SO42 7UF   01590 622246
paul.girling@izrmail.com
www.setleyridge.co.uk

Motor Home & Caravan park

Situated in the New Forest National Park this vineyard, which had been planted some 17 years earlier, was bought by the present owners in 1999 when they found it in a rundown and neglected state. Their decision was to give themselves a complete change of occupation and life style. They immediately set about the refurbishment of the existing and started making alterations and improvements to the facilities and amenities. This included the building, and quipping, of a new winery as well as diversifying the facilities available to the visitors.

Vineyard:
- 6.50 acres under vine
- Between 15 & 30m. above sea level
- Gentle south south-east facing slope
- Sandy loam soil overlying shingle & gravel
- First vines planted in 1982
- Approximately vines to the acre

Winery:
- Still wines – White & Rosé

Farm shop:
- **Open:**
  All year round:
  Daily (09.00 to 17.00)
- **Guided tour & tasting:**
  By appointment only
- **Groups:**
  by prior arrangement only

Features:
- Restaurant
- Garden Centre

Wines: Total wine production of around bottles a year
                Wine sales at Farm Shop & online

Winemaker: Paul Girling

WHITE

Dry White – 2020
- 11.0% – *Aromatic, white flowers & peach/soft acidity & citrus finish*
- Schonburger

ROSÉ

Dry Rosé – 2020
- 12.0% – *Rosé aromas/ripe plum & cherry*
- Rondo, Schonburger

Rosé – 2021
- 12.0% – *Fresh and fruity*
- Rondo

BRIGHTWELL VINEYARD
(Oxfordshire)

Bob & Carol Neilson, Rush Court, Shillingford Road, Wallingford
OX10 8LJ   01491 832354
info@brightwellvineyard.co.uk
www.brightwellvineyard.co.uk

Motor Home Accommodation (Overnight facilities)

The present owners took over this vineyard in 2000 when they bought it from Carol's father Denys Randolph. He had planted the vineyard some 13 years earlier when a number of vineyards were planted in the area. It is to be found on the south bank of the upper River Thames, and with its own small lake, sits in a natural bowl surrounded by the hills of the Chilterns, Cotswolds and North Downs. This location allows the vineyard to benefit from a particular micro-climate in what is probably one of the driest areas in the UK.

Vineyard:
- *16.00 acres under vine*
- *Between 55 & 65m. above sea level*
- *South facing*
- *Flinty chalk and greensand soils*
- *First vines planted in 1987*
- *Approximately 1,400 vines to the acre*

Winery:
- *Sparkling wine – White*
- *Still wines – White, Rosé & Red*

Distillery:
- *Brandy*

Features:
- *Function facilities*
- *Annual Wine Festival (July)*

Cellar Door:
- **Open:**
  All year round
  Saturday & Sunday (12.00 to 18.00)
  Other times:
  By appointment only
- **Guided tours & tasting:**
  June to September:
  When open (11.00 & 16.00)

Wines: Total wine production of around 30,000 bottles a year
Wine sales at Cellar Door, by mail order, at selected local stockists & online

Winemaker: Bob Neilson

SPARKLING

Sparkling Chardonnay – 2010 ◯
- 12.0% – *Classic Method*
- Brut – *(2.0 g/lt) – Zesty hint of apple & lime/citrus tones*
- Chardonnay *(100%)*

WHITE

Bacchus – 2019 ◯
- 12.5% – *Aromatic & fruity/grape flavours & dry finish*
- Bacchus

Oxford Flint – 2019
- 12.5% – *Citrus aftertones/crisp minerality*
- Huxelrebe

Oxford Gold – 2017
- 13.0% – *Mango, pineapple & melon flavours/natural acidity*
- Huxelrebe

ROSÉ

Oxford Rosé – 2018 ◯
- 12.5% – *Ripe cherry flavours/strawberry finish*
- Pinot Noir

RED

Oxford Regatta – 2017 ◯
- 12.0% – *Medium body & fruity/cherry & damson flavours*
- Dornfelder

Pinot Noir – 2016 ◯
- 12.0% – *Cherry, currant & summer berries (barrel aged)*
- Pinot Noir

BRIGHTWELL VINEYARD (OXFORDSHIRE)

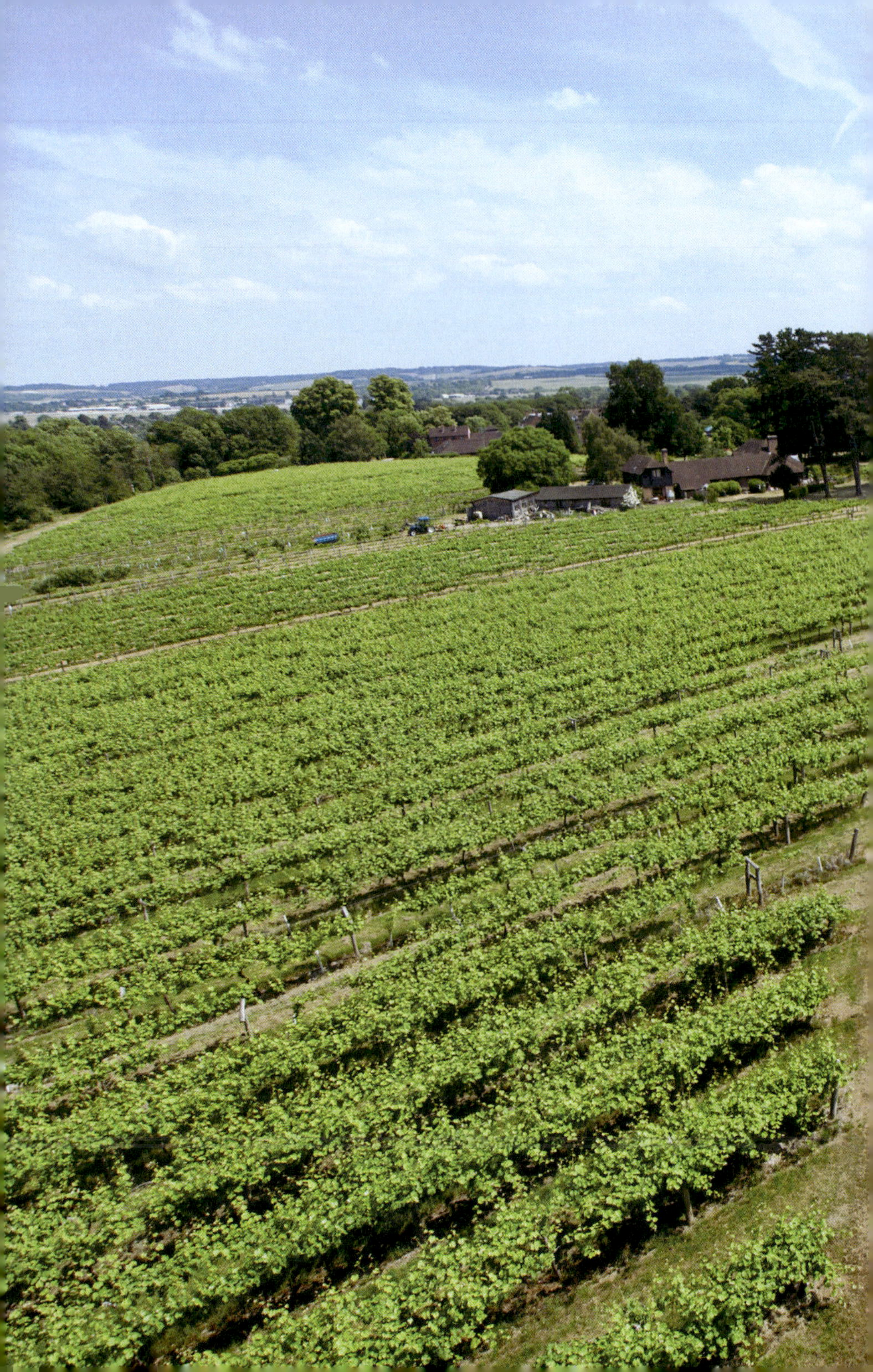

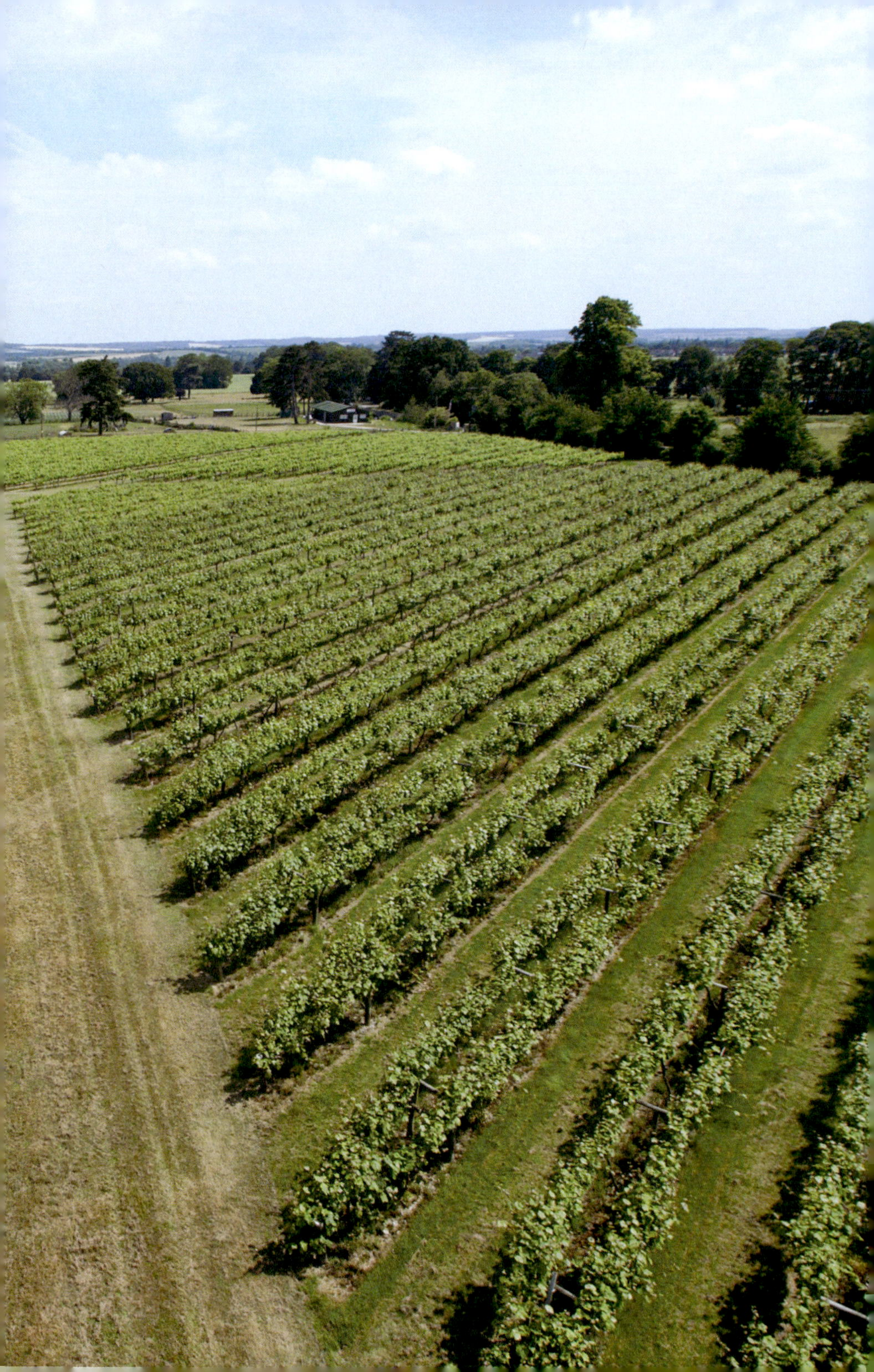

CHILTERN VALLEY VINEYARD
(Oxfordshire)

Donald Ealand
Hambleden, Henley-on-Thames
RG9 6JW   01491 638330
donald@chilternvalley.co.uk
www.chilternvalley.co.uk

1 x 4 bedroom Farmhouse (bed & breakfast) & (dinner)
1 x 2 person Pool House (bed & breakfast) & (dinner)

Formerly known as Old Luxters Vineyard, Winery & Brewhouse. And having its products trading under various labels including Farm Brewery, this vineyard may have changed its name but never its face. It produced its first wine in 1984. It is surrounded by mature Beech woodland and overlooks the Hambleden Valley of the River Thames. The modern winery is located in old brick and flint farm buildings that used to be pig sheds and a grain store. This winery also makes the wines for a number of other local vineyards. A restaurant built in 2000 complements the beautifully restored 17th century barn. These facilities are used when the vineyard often features evenings at the opera.

Vineyard:
- *2.50 acres under vine*
- *Between 183 & 198m. above sea level*
- *Easterly facing slope*
- *Clay & chalky soils*
- *First vines planted in 1982*
- *Approximately 1,200 vines to the acre*

Winery:
- *Sparkling wines – White & Rosé*
- *Still wines – White & Red*

Distillery:
- *Gin*

Brewery:
- *Craft ales*

Cellar Door:
- **Open:**
  All year round
  Daily (09.00 to 17.00)
- **Guided tours & tasting –**
  Monday to Thursday & Saturday (11.00 & 15.00);
  Friday (10.30);
  Sunday (15.00)
- **Groups:**
  By prior arrangement only

Features:
- *Restaurant*
- *Function facilities*

Wines: Total wine production of between 5,000 & 20,000 bottles a year
Wine sales at Cellar Door & online

Winemaker: Donald Ealand

SPARKLING

Sparkling – 2017
- 🛢 12.0% – *Classic Method*
- 🍷 Brut – *(9.0 g/lt) – Dry style*
- 🍇 Madeleine Angevine (%), Seyval Blanc (%)

Sparkling Rosé – 2017
- 🛢 13.0% – *Classic Method*
- 🍷 Brut – *(9.0 g/lt) – Delicate sweetness*
- 🍇 Pinot Noir *(100%)*

WHITE

Black Cat Cuvée - 2015
- 🍷 10.0% – *Rich peach & elderflower hints/citrus flavours*
- 🍇 Ortega, Seyval Blanc

Oaked Seyval - 2015
- 🍷 10.0% – *spiced pear & honeydew melon/citrus & lemon sherbet*
- 🍇 Seyal Blanc

Special Cuvée - 2021
- 🍷 11.0% – *grapefruit aromas/honeyed finish*
- 🍇 Madeleine Angevine, Bacchus

RED

Rondo –2014
- 🍷 12.0% – *earthy aromas/black cherry & plum*
- 🍇 Rondo

CHILTERN VALLEY VINEYARD (OXFORDSHIRE)

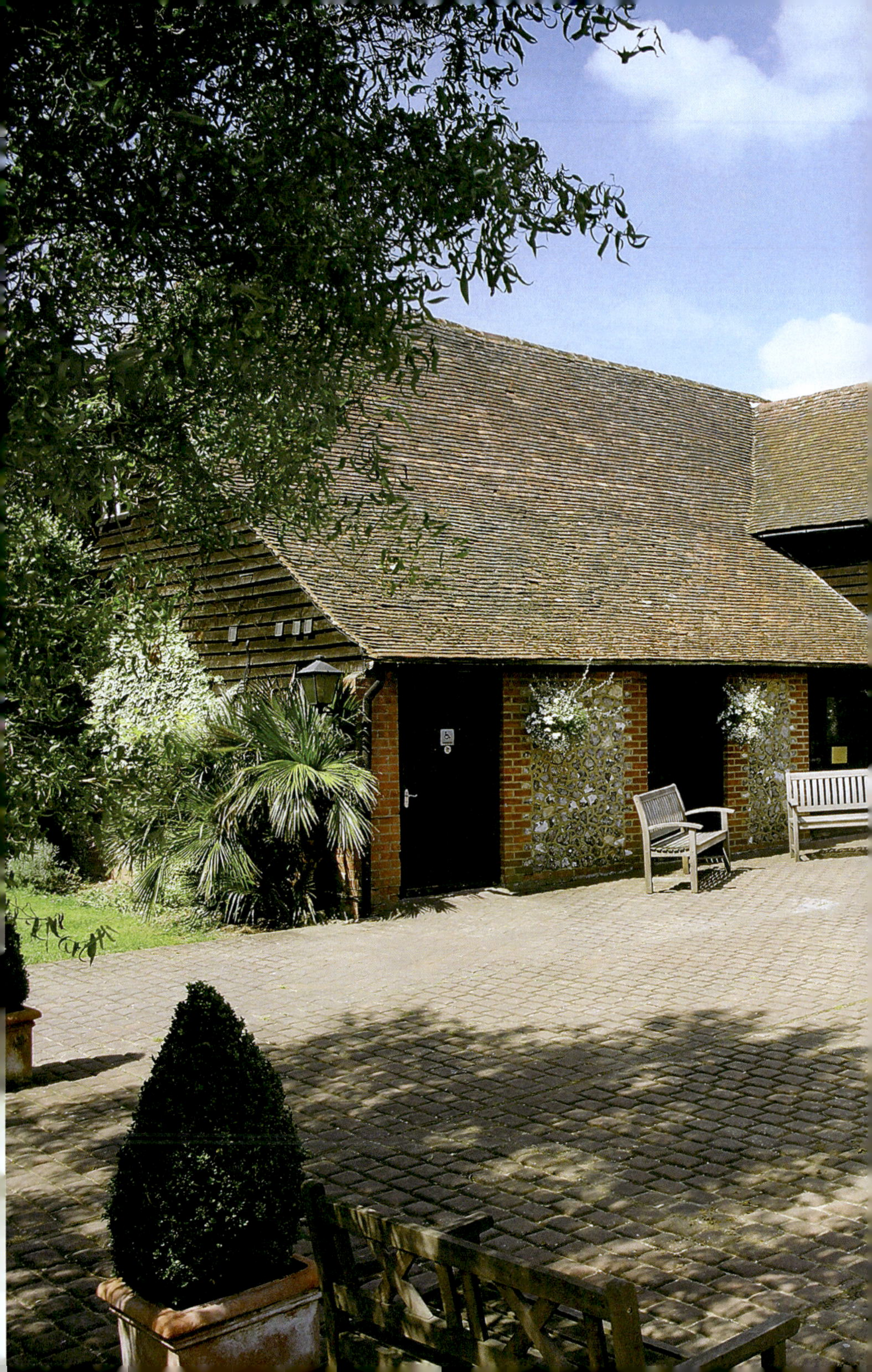

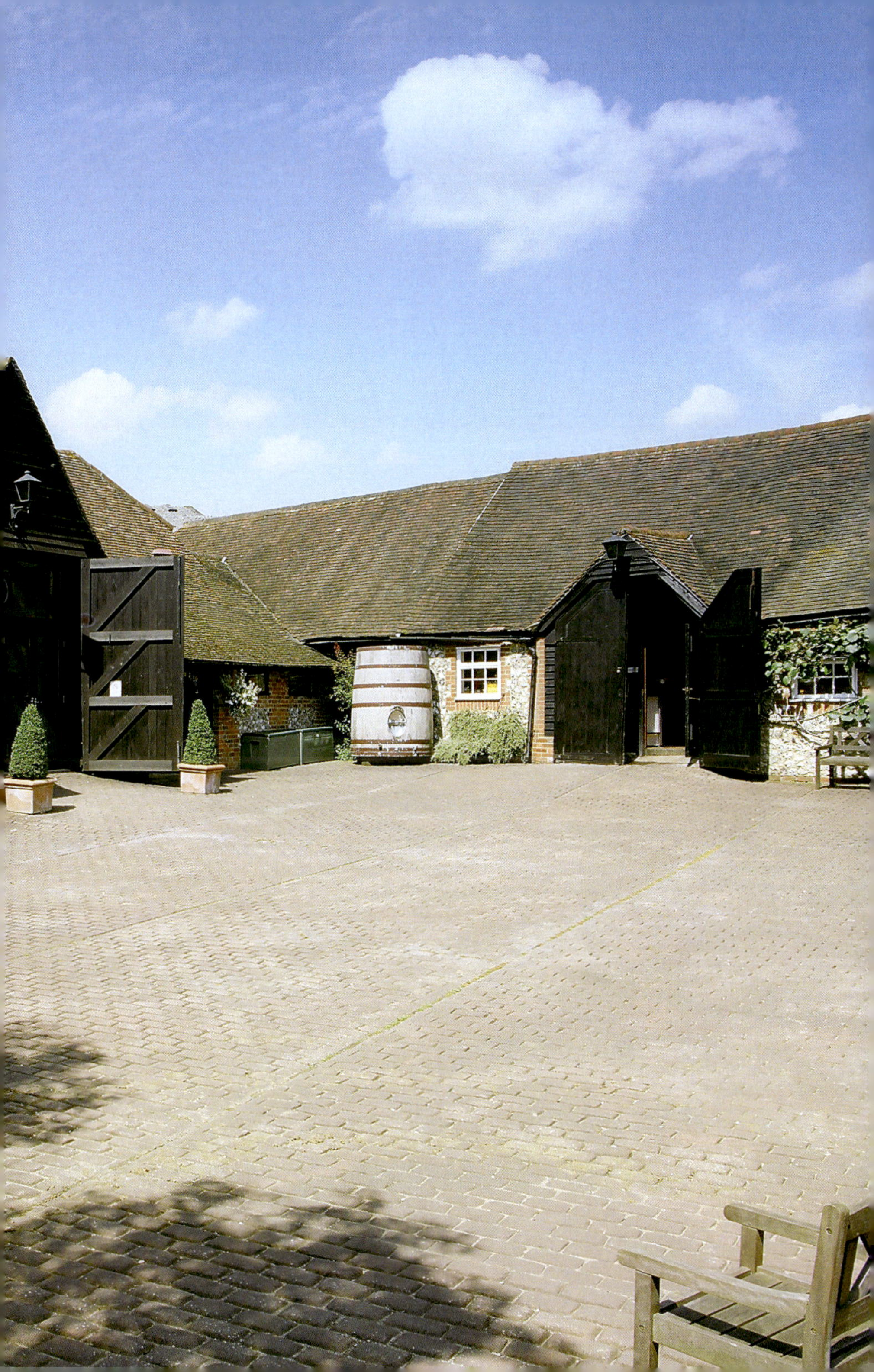

THE SOUTH EAST

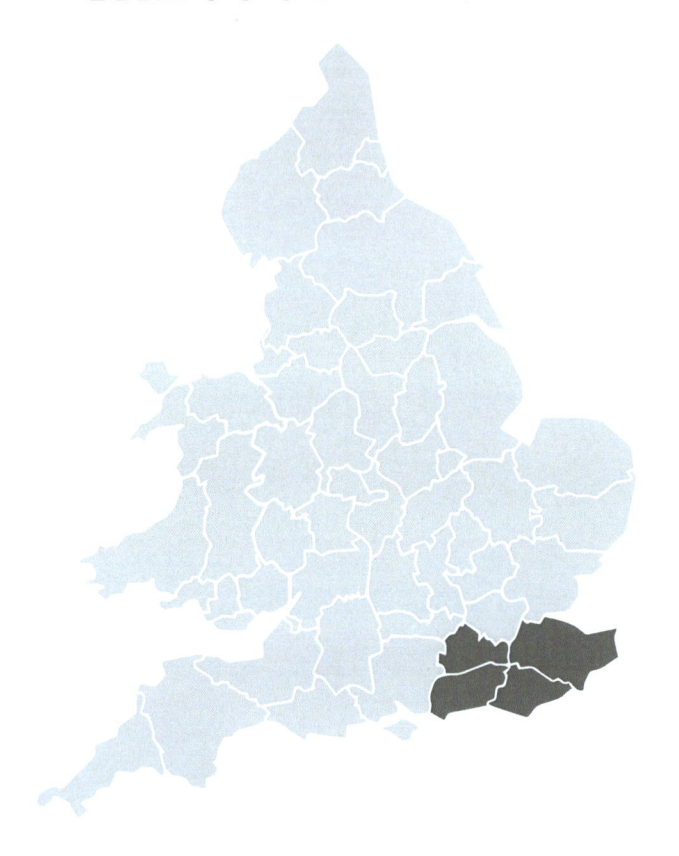

WEST SUSSEX

Ashling Park Estate Vineyard 68

Tinwood Vineyard 70

Kingscote Estate Vineyard 72

Oastbrook Vineyard 74

SURREY

Denbies Wine Estate 78

EAST SUSSEX

Charles Palmer Vineyards 82

Oxney Organic Estate 86

Rathfinny Wine Estate 88

Tillingham Wines (Biodynamic) 90

KENT

Terlingham Vineyard 94

ASHLING PARK ESTATE VINEYARD
A member of **Sussex Modern** (West Sussex)

Gail & Matthew Gardner
Ashling Coach House, Down Street,
West Ashling, PO18 8DP   01243 967700
contact@ashlingpark.co.uk
www.ashlingpark.co.uk

2 x 1 bedroom luxury Lodges
3 x 2 en-suite bedroom luxury Lodges

Within a 50 acre Estate, created in 1822, in the Hamlet of West Ashling, sitting just inside the South Downs National Park, adjacent to the Kingley Vale Nature Reserve and only a short distance from the sea, the present owners decided to create an 11-acre vineyard. The Estate had been presented to Air Marshal Viscount Portal by the UK. Government in recognition of his services during the Second World War as chief of the combined UK and American Bomber Command. After purchasing the Estate in 1995 it took these new owners until 2015 to make the decision to plant a vineyard came after careful consideration of the suitability of the farm soils and this micro-climate. Up until that date it had been a family arable farm. The first vines were planted in what had been a hay meadow. Protected by 100 year old mature oak trees, on the adjacent slopes, the vineyard is able to benefit from its own particular micro-climate which has higher than the regional average for sunlight and lower than the regional average for frost being just 1 mile from the sea. The vineyard now incorporates many and various other activities and features including the production of its own honey, and other wax based products, from its many bee hives and having its own ornamental lake. And for those fortunate enough it has its own helipad.

Vineyard:
- 33 acres under vine
- Between 20 & 30m. above sea level
- First vines planted in 2015
- South west facing slope
- Loamy soil on limestone/chalk base
- Approximately 2,000 vines to the acre

- Sparkling wines – White & Rosé
- Still wines – Rosé

Distillery:
- Gin
- Rum

Apiary:
- Honey

Visitors' Centre:
- **Open:**
All year round:
Thursday to Sunday
Other times:
By appointment only
- **Guided tour & tastings:**
Thursday to Sunday (10.30 & 14.00)
By appointment only

Features:
- *Gin distilling course*
- *Bee keeping course*
- *Helipad (by arrangement)*
- *Restaurant*
- *Function facilities*
- *Social activities*

Wines: Total wine production of around 20,000 bottles a year
Wine sales at Visitors' Centre, at selected stockists & online

Winemaker: Dermot Sugrue (at Wiston Estate); Nick Lane (at Defined Wines)

SPARKLING

Blanc de Blancs – 2014 ()
- 12.0% – *Classic Method*
- Brut – *(10.0 g/lt) – Hedgerow blossom & incisive citrus fruit/hint of yellow plums*
- Chardonnay *(100%)*

Cuvée – NV ()
- 12.0% – *Classic Method*
- Brut – *(8.0 g/lt) – Crisp & precise/ white flowers, ripe stone fruit & soft acidity*
- Pinot Noir, Chardonnay, Pinot Meunier

Sparkling Rosé – 2014 ()
- 12.0% – *Classic Method*
- Brut – *(8.0 g/lt) – Dry, crisp & fresh/plums, rhubarb & autumn fruits*
- Pinot Noir, Pinot Meunier

ROSÉ

Rosé – 2020 ()
- 12.0% – *Red apple & thyme/zesty pink grapefruit*
- Pinot Meunier

ASHLING PARK ESTATE VINEYARD (WEST SUSSEX)

TINWOOD VINEYARD
(West Sussex)

Art Tukker
Tinwood Lane, Halnaker, PO18 0NE
01243 537372
info@tinwoodestate.com
www.tinwoodestate.com

8 x 1-bedroom Luxury Lodges (bed & breakfast)

Sitting at the foot of the South Downs National Park, and adjacent to the Goodwood Estate, the vineyard benefits from being in a rain shadow and having its own particular micro-climate. It is only three miles from the sea as the crow flies. The vineyard is located on the family farm which was acquired in 1985 as an Iceberg lettuce producing one. When the first vines were planted the direction of agricultural life changed. This planting was carried out by the 2nd generation of the family and who are now the owners. The vineyard is environmentally friendly with flowers planted between the rows of vines to encourage the bees from the on farm apiaries.

Vineyard:

- *65.00 acres under vine*
- *Around 35m. above sea level*
- *South westerly aspect*
- *Stoney soil over chalk*
- *First vines planted in 2007*
- *Approximately 1,700 vines to the acre*

- *Sparkling wines – White & Rosé*

Apiary:

- *Honey*

Visitors' Centre:

- **Open:**
  All year round:
  Daily (10.00 to 18.00)
- **Guided tour & tasting:**
  Weekdays (15.00);
  Saturday & Sunday (12.00 & 15.00)

Wines:
Total wine production of around 30,000 bottles a year
Wine sales at Visitors' Centre, at selected stockists & online

Winemakers:
Simon Roberts (at Ridgeview Estate) & Art Tukker

SPARKLING

Blanc de Blancs – 2019 ()
- 12.0% – *Classic Method*
- Brut – *(7.5 g/lt) – Green apple apples/tropical fruit & soft minerality*
- Chardonnay *(100%)*

Blanc de Noir – 2018
- 12.0% – *Classic Method*
- Brut – *(g/lt) – Toasty biscuit & blackcurrant/balanced acidity*
- Pinot Noir *(%)*, Pinot Meunier *(%)*

Brut – 2019
- 12.0% – *Classic Method*
- Brut – *(7.5 g/lt) – Citrus & melon/ hints of honey & brioche*
- Chardonnay *(50%)*, Pinot Noir *(30%)*, Pinot Meunier *(20%)*

Rosé – 2019 ()
- 12.0% – *Classic Method*
- Brut – *(10.0 g/lt) – Red forest fruits/ raspberries & strawberries&cream*
- Pinot Noir *(60%)*, Pinot Meunier *(20%)*, Chardonnay *(20%)*

TINWOOD VINEYARD (WEST SUSSEX)

KINGSCOTE ESTATE VINEYARD
(West Sussex)

Ellie Coleridge, Mill Place Farm,
Vowels Lane, Kingscote,
RH19 4LG   01342 327535
info@kingscoteestate.com
www.kingscoteestate.com

1 x 2 person holiday Cottage (self-catering)

This vineyard is a short picturesque cross country walk from the Kingscote station on the Heritage railway Bluebell Line. It forms part of an Estate, situated within the Wealden Valley, of 150 acres that dates back at least to the early 14th century when its first recorded event was that of building a timber framed Iron Master's Hall in 1320. The Estate, part of which is designated as a 'Site of Special Scientific Interest', includes a winding section of the River Medway and well stocked fishing lakes and is set amongst rolling hills. In 1884 the Estate, along with Gravetye Manor, was bought by William Robinson, the 'Grand Old Man' of the New Gardening Movement, who then proceeded to create a picturesque landscape. A later owner, Christen Monge, bought the Estate in 1990 and continued the gardening philosophy together with extending the principles of the Estate by planting a vineyard in 2010. After the sudden death of Christen, Mark Dixon took over the Estate in 2015 and added it to his portfolio of English and French vineyards. He proceeded to enlarge the original 20 acre vineyard to its present size and also commenced converting the vineyard into an organic one. Within the Estate the existing 15th-century Tithe Barn has been fully restored and has now become the Visitors' Centre. Traditional crafts are maintained within the sparkling wine making process with some bottles still being hand riddled.

Vineyard:
- 60 acres under vine
- Between 70 & 80m. above sea level
- South facing slopes
- Sandy, clay & ironstone soils
- First vines planted in 2010
- Approximately 1,700 vines to the acre

Winery:
- Sparkling wines – White & Rosé
- Still wines – White & Rosé

Visitors' Centre:
- **Open:**
  All year round:
  April to September:
  Daily (10.00 to 17.00)
- **Guided tour & tasting:**
  Thursday to Sunday (10.00, 12.00, 14.00 & 16.00)
- **Self-guided walkabout:**
  When open
- **Groups:**
  By prior arrangement only

Features:
- Fishing
- Function facilities

Wines: Total wine production of around 150,000 bottles a year
Wine sales at Visitors' Centre & online

Winemaker: Theo Cullen

SPARKLING

Brut – NV
- 11.5% – *Classic Method*
- Brut – *(g/lt) – Kitchen garden, gooseberry & apple/hints of rosé*
- Pinot Meunier, Chardonnay

Brut – 2018
- 11.5% – *Charmat Method*
- Brut – *(g/lt) – Elderflower & gooseberry aromas/grassy notes & bright mousse*
- Bacchus *(%)*, Pinot Meunier *(%)*, Chardonnay *(%)*

Rosé Brut – NV
- 12.0% – *Classic Method*
- Brut – *(g/lt) – Raspberry, strawberry & shortbread/summer fruits & fresh acidity*
- Pinot Meunier, Pinot Noir

Rosé Brut 2019
- 11.5% – *Charmat Method*
- Brut – *(g/lt) – Subtle aromas of citrus & red fruits*
- Bacchus *(%)*, Pinot Noir *(%)*, Pinot Meunier *(%)*, Chardonnay *(%)*

WHITE

Bacchus – 2019
- 11.5% – *Floral nose/elderflower, apple, gooseberry & crisp finish*
- Bacchus

Silvan Bacchus – 2019
- 11.5% – *Rich, creamy & indulgent/soft acidity*
- Bacchus

Chardonnay – 2019
- 11.0% – *Aromatic, rich & buttery/lemon sherbet & green apple*
- Chardonnay

ROSÉ

The Rosé – 2018
- 10.5% – *Floral elderflower & citrus/ripe peaches, raspberries & strawberries*
- Bacchus, Regent

KINGSCOTE ESTATE VINEYARD (WEST SUSSEX)

OASTBROOK VINEYARD
A member of **Rother Valley Vineyards** *(West Sussex)*

America & Nick Brewer
Park Farm Oast, Junction Road, Bodiam,
TN32 5XA   01580 854647
info@oastbrook.com
www.oastbrook.com

1 x 2 bedroom Halfling House (self-catering)
1 x 2 bedroom 'A' frame waterside House (self-catering)
Glamping facilities

On a 60 acre Estate farm, located in the River Rother valley and just a short walk from Bodiam Castle, that had been owned by the Guinness company as a hop farm, these new owners quickly established a vineyard. The micro-climate of the site and surrounds appeared to be most suitable for growing of vines. These owners had spent many years in Hong Kong so this establishment of a vineyard was a completely new venture for them. The recently planted vines are now producing their first crops which will be vinified in the vineyard's newly built and equipped winery.

Vineyard:
- *12.00 acres under vine*
- *Around 11m. above sea level*
- *South facing slopes*
- *Clay silt soil over sandstone*
- *First vines planted in 2018*
- *Approximately 1,600 vines to the acre*

Winery:
- *Sparkling wine – Rosé & white*
- *Still wines – White, Rosé & Red*

Visitors' Centre:
- **Open:**
  All year round:
  Tuesday to Thursday (10.00 to 18.00);
  Friday to Sunday (10.00 to 21.00)

Features:
- *Wine based events*
- *Theatrical performances*
- *Function facilities*
- *Licensed for civil ceremonies*

Wines:
Total wine production of around 50,000 to 60,000 bottles a year
Wine sales at Visitors' Centre & online

Winemakers:
Nick & America Brewer
Dermot Sugrue (at Wiston Estate)

SPARKLING

Rosé – 2015 ◐
- 12.0% – *Classic Method*
- Brut – *(8.0 g/lt) – Forest fruits & brioche/ripe red fruits, winter spice & strawberry shortcake*
- Pinot Noir *(50%)*, Chardonnay *(30%)*, Pinot Meunier *(20%)*

Cuvée – 2014
- 12.0% – *Classic Method*
- Brut – *(7.8 g/lt) – Lemon, pear, apple & brioche/hints of shortbread*
- Chardonnay *(62%)*, Pinot Noir *(21%)*, Pinot Meunier *(17%)*

WHITE

Pinot Gris – 2020
- 12.0% – *Peach, nectarine & elderflower/elegant minerality*
- Pinot Gris

Chardonnay – 2022
- 12.0% – *Yellow plum, pear drops & vanilla/honeysuckle*
- Chardonnay

Chardonnay Reserve – 2021
- 12.0% – *Peach, apricot & white apple/vanilla, toast, coconut & honey*
- Chardonnay

Pinot Blanc – 2022
- 12.0% – *Apple, pear & stone fruit/ white peach & nectarine*
- Pinot Blanc

Pinot Meunier – 2022
- 12.0% – *Raspberry, strawberry & black fruits/ creamy mouth feel*
- Pinot Meunier

ROSÉ

Rosé Reserve – 2022
- 12.0% – *Cherry, raspberry & peach/ cranberry, lemon, grapefruit & ripe breadfruit*
- Pinot Noir

RED

Pinot Noir – 2020
- 12.0% – *Strawberry, cranberry & raspberry liquor/toasted brioche*
- Pinot Noir

Pinot Noir Reserve – 2021
- 12.0% – *Summer red fruit & orange rind/vanilla toast, creme caramel & slight spice*
- Pinot Noir

OASTBROOK VINEYARD (WEST SUSSEX)

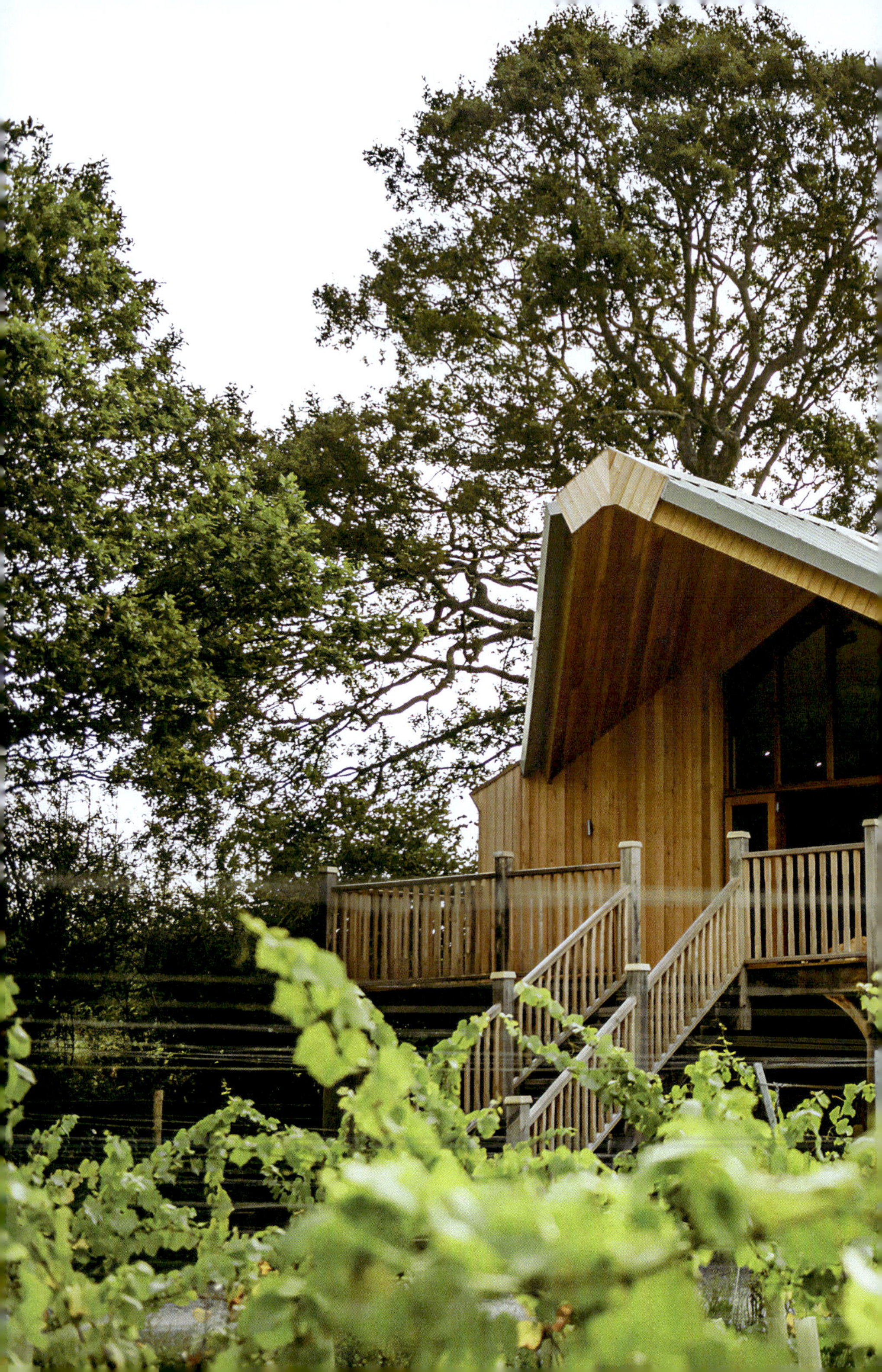

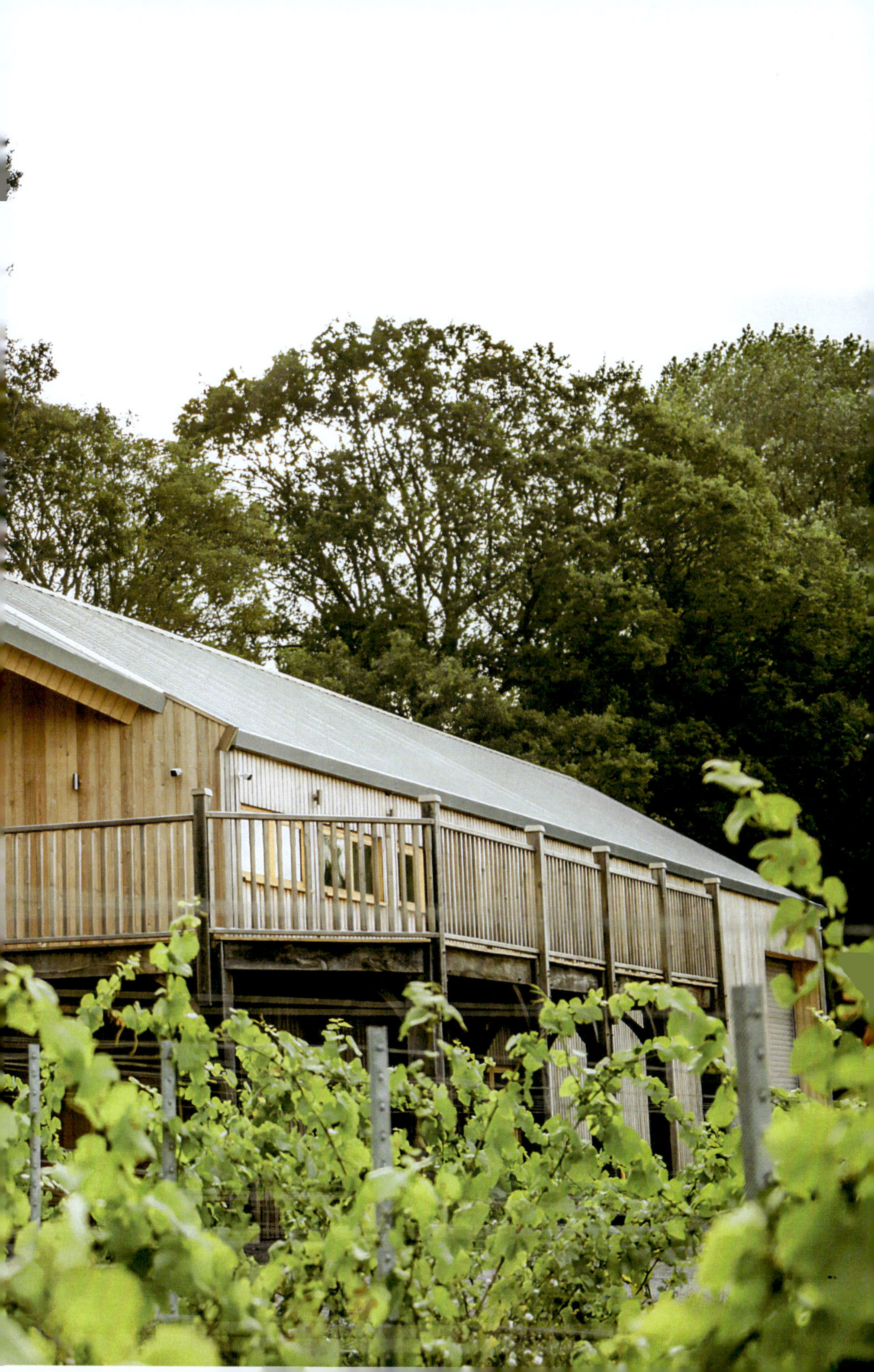

DENBIES WINE ESTATE
A member of **Vineyards of the Surrey Hills** *(Surrey)*

Janette Simpson
London Road, Dorking, RH5 6AA
01306 876616
jsimpson@denbiesvineyard.co.uk
www.denbies.co.uk

17 en-suite bedroom
Hotel (bed & breakfast)

When referred to in the Doomsday Book of William I, the Estate was considerably larger in area than it is now. Historically the area was known for its wine production in Roman times and has also been mentioned in early 18th century literature. A local industrialist bought the Estate, in 1984, with the intention of having an intensive cattle and pig fattening enterprize. This became unviable under EU regulations. Professional advice was then sought, from Dr Richard Selly of Imperial College, and considering the soil and topographical advantages of this area of the South Downs it was decided to plant a vineyard. The present day vineyard, which came into theownership of the present owner in 2001, is believed to be the largest single site vineyard in the UK and forms part of a 617 acre well wooded estate. It was planted over a seven year period as a continuous endeavour by the present owner's father. The now long established vineyard is well organised for visitors with the guided tour of the vineyard being by Land Rover hauled 'road train' and that of the winery by 'people mover'. There is also a well marked walk, comprising of nearly seven miles on various paths, around the vineyard, with various vantage points, for those who want this serious up- and downhill hike. The newly built, and recently opened, hotel forms yet another attraction.

Vineyard:

- *265.00 acres under vine*
- *Between 50 & 100m. above sea level*
- *East & south facing slopes*
- *Fertile flinty loam over chalky strata*
- *First vines planted in 1986*
- *Approximately 1,150 vines to the acre*

Winery:

- *Sparkling wines – White & Rosé*
- *Still wines – White, Rosé & Red*

Visitors' Centre:

- **Open:**
  April to December:
  Monday to Saturday (09.30 to 17.30);
  Sunday (10.00 to 17.30)
  January to March:
  Monday to Saturday (09.30 to 17.00);
  Sunday (10.00 to 17.30)
- **Guided tours & tasting:**
  All year round:
  Daily (on the hour)
- **Self-guided walkabout:**
  When open
- **Groups**
  By prior arrangement only

Features:
- Art gallery
- Farm Shop
- Selected events
- Restaurant
- Function facilities
- Licensed for civil ceremonies

Wines:
Total wine production of around 1,000,000 bottles a year
Wine sales at Visitors' Centre, at local & national stockists & online

Winemakers: John Worontschak & Matthieu Elzinga

SPARKLING

Bacchus – 2019 ()
- 11.5% – *Classic Method*
- Brut – *(5.0 g/lt) – Honeysuckle, red fruits & rosé petal/zingy citrus fruit acidity & creamy finish*
- Bacchus *(100%)*

Whitedowns – NV
- 12.0% – *Classic Method*
- Brut – *(9.0 g/lt) – Citrus aromas & hint of brioche/creamy texture & balanced acidity*
- Rondo, Seyval Blanc, Pinot Noir

Greenfields – NV ()
- 12.5% – *Classic Method*
- Brut – *(8.0 g/lt) – Yeasty complexity, brioche & strawberry notes/hints of vanilla & lavender*
- Pinot Noir, Pinot Meunier, Chardonnay

Cubitt Reserve Blanc de Noirs – 2014
- 12.0% – *Classic Method*
- Brut – (4.2 g/lt) – *Baked pear & rose petal aromas/strawberries & mineral crisp acidity*
- Pinot Noir (100%)

Cubitt Reserve Blanc de Blancs – 2014
- 12.5% – *Classic Method*
- Brut – (4.0 g/lt) –
- Chardonnay (100%)

Sparkling Bacchus – 2016
- 12.5% – *Classic Method*
- Brut – (5.0 g/lt) – *Fresh honeysuckle, red fruits & rose petal/zingy fruit acidity*
- Bacchus (100%)

Demi-Sec – NV
- 12.0% – *Classic Method*
- Demi-Sec – (48.0 g/lt) – *Aromas of brioche & pear/honeysuckle & sweet apple*
- Reichensteiner, Seyval Blanc

Whitedowns Rosé – NV
- 12.5% – *Classic Method*
- Brut – (7.2 g/lt) – *Fresh fruit & dried cranberries/smooth mousse*
- Chardonnay, Pinot Blanc, Pinot Noir, Seyval Blanc

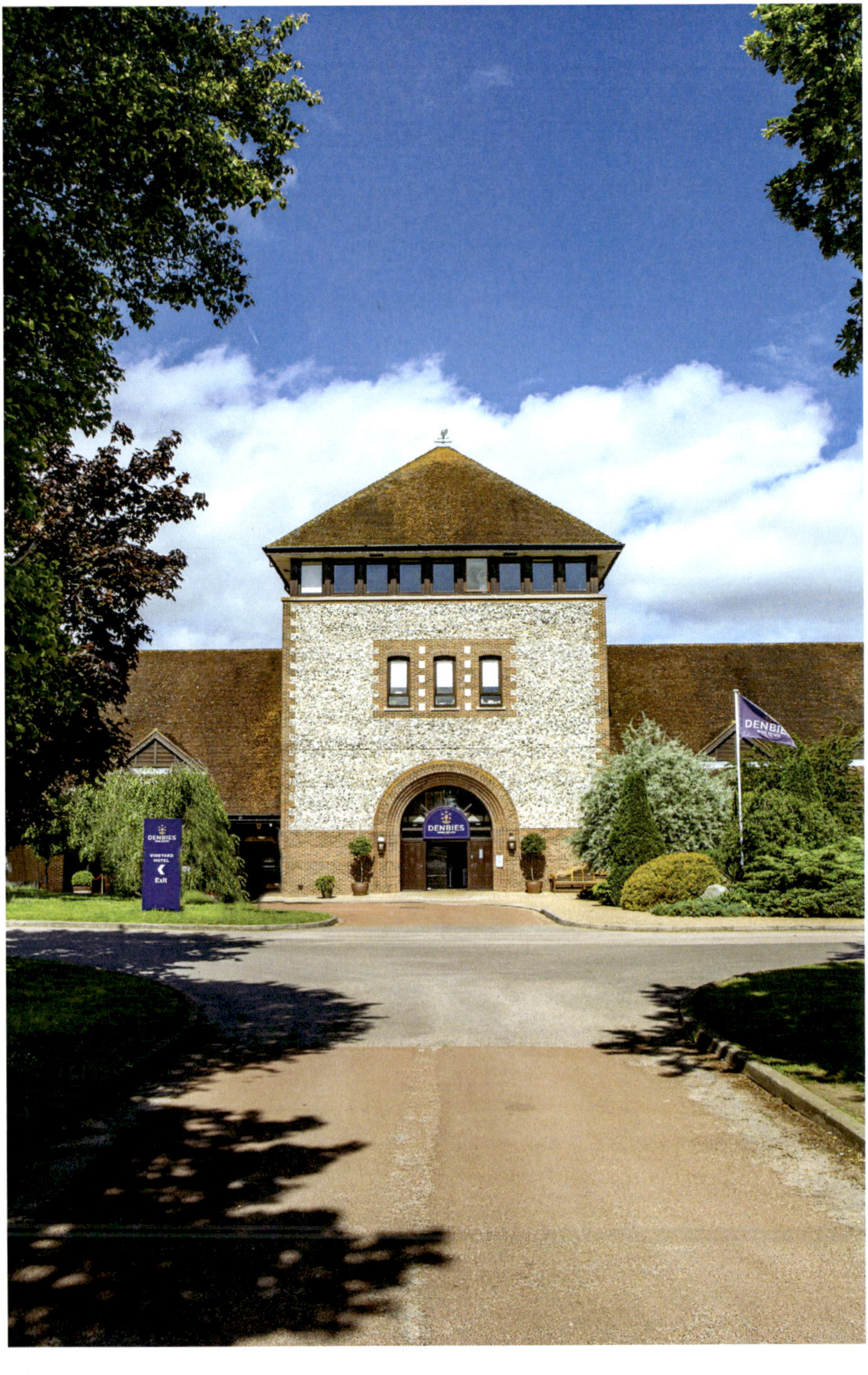
DENBIES
VINEYARD HOTEL
Exit
DENBIES
DENBIES

WHITE

Flint Valley – NV
- 11.5% – *Lime zest & ripe pear/fresh citrus & refreshing minerality*
- Seyval Blanc

Bacchus – 2019
- 12.0% – *Gooseberry & elderflower/ summer fruits & hints of English hedgerow*
- Bacchus

Ranmore Hill – 2018 ()
- 12.0% – *Creamy pear & melon notes/buttery hints of ripe red apple*
- Chardonnay, Pinot Gris, Bacchus

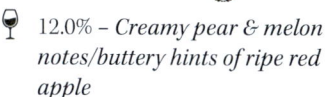

Chardonnay – 2020
- 12.0% – *Ripe fruit & baked apple/ buttered toast*
- Chardonnay

ROSÉ

Rosé Hill –
- 12.0% – *Nose of summer fruits/ strawberris, raspberries, toffee apple & cassis*
- Dornfelder, Pinot Noir

RED

Redlands –
- 12.0% – *Strawberries, raspberries & hints of vanilla/red berry fruits & velvety texture*
- Dornfelder, Rondo, Pinot Noir

Pinot Noir – 2019
- 12.0% – *Plum & late summer raspberries/spicy cinnamon*
- Pinot Noir

ORANGE

Orange Solaris – 2021
- 12.0% – *Apricot stone fruit/baked apple & tangerine*
- Solaris

DENBIES WINE ESTATE (SURREY)

CHARLES PALMER VINEYARDS
A member of **Rother Valley Vineyards** *(East Sussex)*

Robert Palmer, Wickham Manor,
Wickham Rock Lane, Winchelsea
TN36 4AD   01797 226216
charles@charlespalmer-vineyards.co.uk
www.charlespalmer-vineyards.co.uk

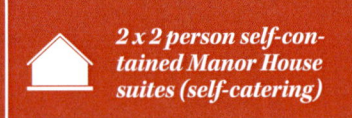

2 x 2 person self-contained Manor House suites (self-catering)

This vineyard is located near to the sea and open to its climatic influences by being almost at sea level. Planted in the grounds of the 16th century Manor House that is the Palmer family home, and overlooking the Brede valley, it is a family run and operated vineyard that is proud of its dedication to wine making. The completion of the on-site winery in 2017, in a converted grain store, enabled all the winemaking to be carried out by the family at home. Other Estate buildings are being, or have been, converted into other facilities for the vineyard use. The Cellar Door is in a converted stable block. With these influences of climatic variation, and the unique terroir, each vintage has its own individual and unique character.

Vineyard:
- *35.00 acres under vine*
- *Between 3 & 30m. above sea level*
- *South facing slopes*
- *Soil over Kimmeridge clay*
- *First vines planted in 2006*
- *Approximately 750 vines to the acre*

Winery:
- *Sparkling wines – White & Rosé*
- *Still wines – White, Rosé & Red*

Features:
- *Themed events*

Cellar Door:
- **Open:**
  All year round:
  Wednesday to Saturday
  (11.00 to 17.00);
  Sunday (12.00 to 16.00)
- **Guided tour & tasting:**
  Wednesday to Saturday
  (11.00, 13.00 & 15.00);
  Sunday (12.00 & 14.00)
  By appointment only
- **Self-guided walkabout:**
  When open

Wines: Total wine production of around 50,000 bottles a year
           Wine sales at Cellar Door, at local stockists & online

Winemakers: Charles & Robert Palmer, Will Davenport

SPARKLING

Special Reserve – 2012
- 12.0% – *Classic Method*
- Brut – *(9.0 g/lt) – Ripe apricots, toasted almonds/biscuit & hints of blackberry*
- Pinot Noir *(100%)*

Classic Cuvée – 2016
- 12.0% – *Classic Method*
- Brut – *(9.0 g/lt) – Honey & fig/lemon sherbet & minerality*
- Chardonnay *(70%)*, Pinot Noir *(30%)*

Blanc de Blancs – 2016
- 12.0% – *Classic Method*
- Brut – *(11.0 g/lt) – Gooseberry, grapefruit & butter pastry/pear*
- Chardonnay *(100%)*

Demi-Sec – 2016
- 12.0% – *Classic Method*
- Demi-Sec – *(32.0 g/lt) – Peaches & apricots/smooth taste of nectar*
- Pinot Noir *(60%)*, Chardonnay *(40%)*

Rosé – 2017
- 12.0% – *Classic Method*
- Brut – *(6.0 g/lt) – Red apple/shortbread, red berries & raspberry*
- Pinot Noir *(100%)*

WHITE

Chardonnay – 2018
- 11.5% – *Lime aromas/pear, baked apple & white peach*
- Chardonnay

ROSÉ

Rosé – 2018
- 12.0% – *Floral hints/red cherry, cranberry & raspberry*
- Pinot Noir

RED

Pinot Noir – 2019
- 12.0% – *(Lightly oaked) – Violets & hibiscous/cranberry, raspberry & cherry*
- Pinot Noir

CHARLES PALMER VINEYARDS (EAST SUSSEX)

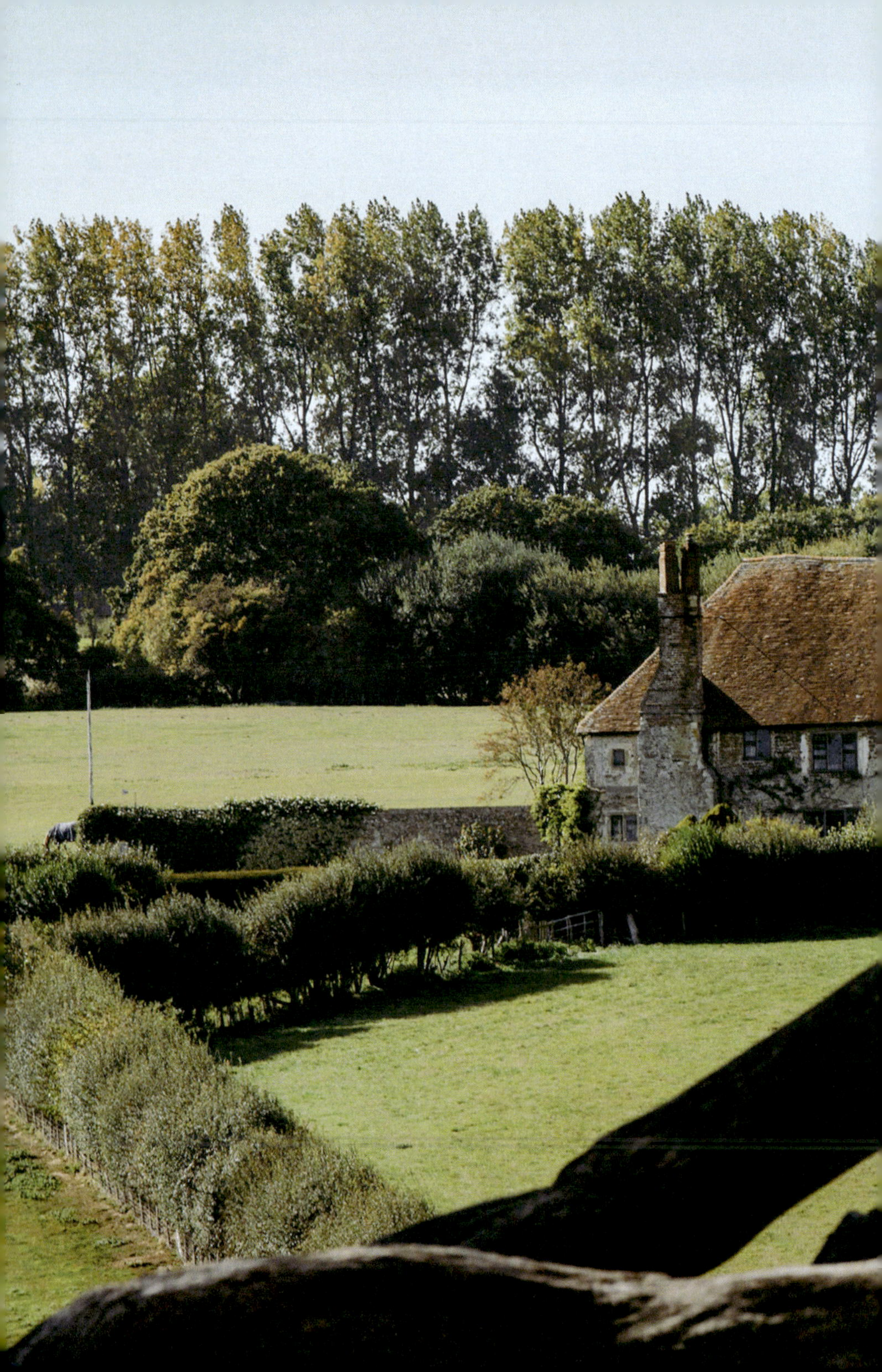

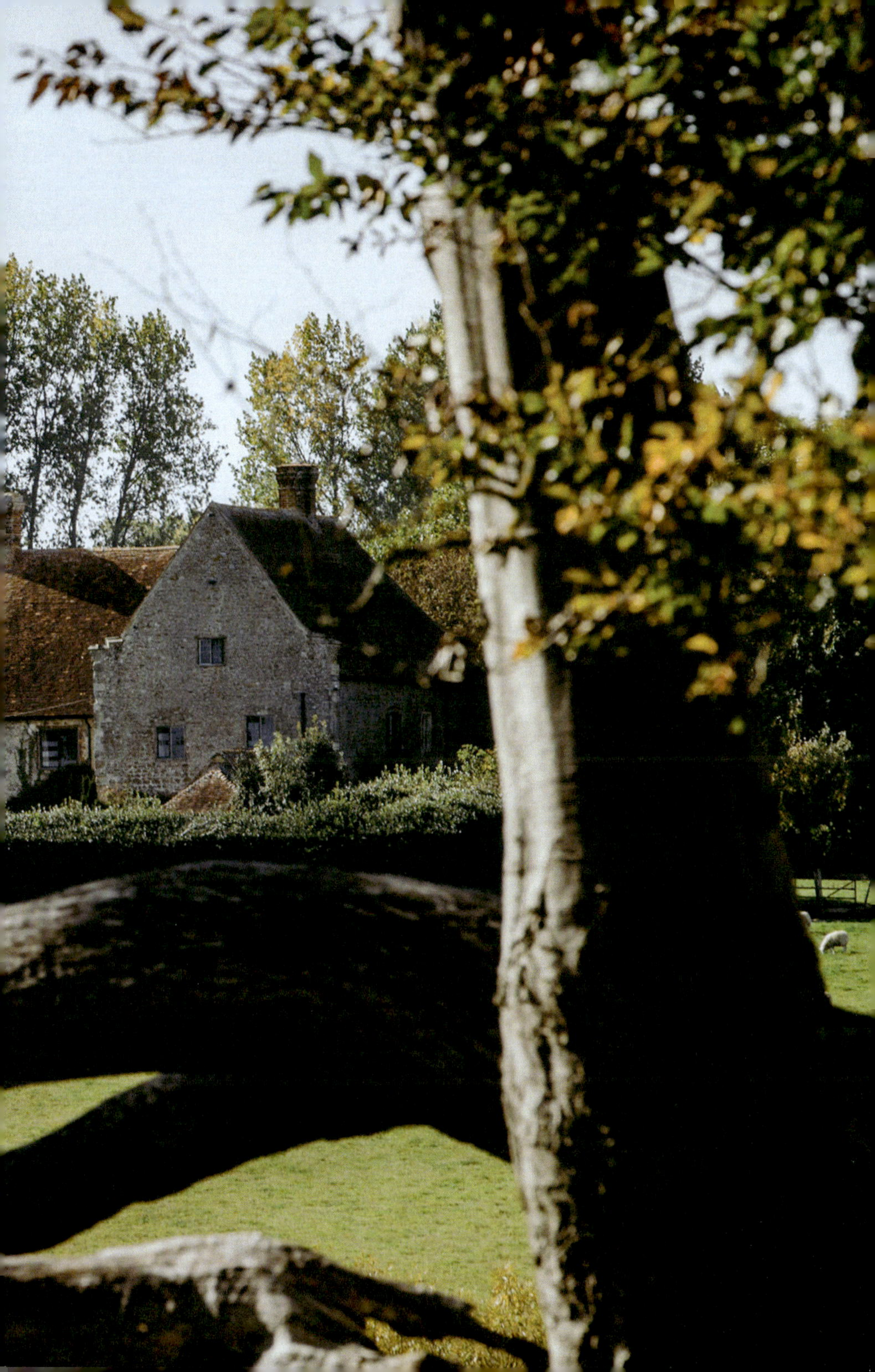

OXNEY ORGANIC ESTATE
A member of **Rother Valley Vineyards, Sussex Modern & Visit 1066**
(East Sussex)

Kristin Syltevik & Paul Dobson
Little Bellhurst Farm, Hobbs Lane,
Beckley, TN31 6TU   01797 260137
wine@oxneyestate.com
www.oxneyestate.com

1 x 7 bedroom converted Barn (self-catering)
1 x 3 bedroom Farm House (self-catering)
2 x 2 person Shepherd's Huts (self-catering)

The 800 acre farm that forms this Estate was first mentioned in the Doomsday Book of 1086 when it consisted of many small walled fields. These have now been opened out into the present organic arable farm and coppiced woodland. These present owners moved in in 2009. Within the Estate one small parcel of 21 acres was developed as a vineyard. This parcel has now been extended to create a vineyard of its present size and make it the largest single site organic vineyard in the UK. The vineyard slopes down to the River Rother and the total farm Estate overlooks the river's flood plane. The vineyard also benefits from its own micro-climate being in an area of low rainfall. The modern winery is located within a Grade II listed converted square oast house and many of the other vineyard facilities are to be found in restored old farm buildings. The Farm House probably dates back to the 17th century. The Estate is managed on sustainable principles.

Vineyard:
- 35.00 acres under vine
- Around 17m. above sea level
- South west facing slope
- Silt loam soil & Tunbridge Wells sand
- First vines planted in 2012
- Approximately 1,500 vines to the acre

Winery:
- Sparkling wine – White
- Still wines – White, Rosé & Red

Cider Press:
- Sparkling cider

Cellar Door:
- **Open:**
  April to October:
  Monday to Friday (10.00 to 16.00)
  By appointment only
  Saturday (10.00 to 16.00)
- **Guided tour & tasting:**
  April to October:
  Saturday (11.00)
- **Groups:**
  By prior arrangement only

Wines: Total wine production of between 23,000 & 34,000 bottles a year
            Wine sales at Cellar Door, at local & national stockists & online

Winemaker: Salvatore Leone

SPARKLING

Classic – 2018 ◯
- 12.0% – *Classic Method*
- Brut – *(5.0 g/lt) – Ripe orchard fruit aromas/biscuit, brioche notes & crisp acidity*
- Pinot Meunier *(47%)*, Pinot Noir *(45%)*, Chardonnay *(8%)*

Estate – NV
- 11.0% – *Classic Method*
- Brut – *(9.0 g/lt) – Fresh & crisp/red apple, pear & toast*
- Chardonnay, Pinot Noir, Pinot Meunier, Seyval Blanc

Classic Chardonnay 2018
- % – *Classic Method*
- Brut – *(g/lt) –*
- Chardonnay *(100%)*

River Cottage – NV
- % – *Classic Method*
- Brut – *(g/lt) – Toasty orchard fruit flavours*

Classic Rosé 2019
- % – *Classic Method*
- Brut – *(0.0 g/lt) –*
- Pinot Noir *(100%)*

WHITE

Chardonnay – 2020
- 12.5% – *Stone fruit, hazelnut & toast aromas/citrus zest, nuts & butterscotch*
- Chardonnay

ROSÉ

Pinot Noir Rosé – 2020
- 12.5% – *Lifted raspberry, cranberry & rhubarb notes/citrus & red berry*
- Pinot Noir

RED

Pinot Noir Red – 2020
- 12.5% –
- Pinot Noir

OXNEY ORGANIC ESTATE (EAST SUSSEX)

RATHFINNY WINE ESTATE
A member of **Sussex Wineries Partnership** *(East Sussex)*

Mark & Sarah Driver
Alfriston, BN28 5TL
01323 871031
info@rathfinnyestate.com
www.rathfinnyestate.com

10 en-suite bedrooms
(bed & breakfast)

This vineyard is situated within the Cradle Valley, straddling the river, and overlooking the South Downs National Park. With a view of the sea that is only three miles away at a distance that the Romans thought ideal for growing vines, it comprises just over half of this 600 acre Estate. The Estate, which had been an arable farm, was spotted for sale by Sarah, in 2010, just as her husband Mark had enrolled on the foundation degree course at Plumpton College. One particular part of the Estate has been planted with banks of trees to provide helpful wind breaks for the vineyard and this combined with the other features allows it to benefit from its own micro-climate. The land that forms the remainder of the Estate is open to roam around. The total acreage of vines is continuing to rise and has been accompanied by the newly built accommodation building, a nominated RIBA award winery and other facilities. This total development has enabled the vineyard to be self-sufficient and energy efficient in all aspects of the wine producing process.

Vineyard:
- *350.00 acres under vine*
- *Between m. above sea level*
- *South facing slopes*
- *Silty clay loam soil over chalk*
- *First vines planted in 2012*
- *Approximately 1,640 vines to the acre*

Winery:
- *Sparkling wines – White & Rosé*

Distillery:
- *Gin*
- *Vermouth*

Visitors' Centre:
- **Open:**
  All year round:
  Daily (10.00 to 16.00)
- **Guided tour & tasting:**
  April & May:
  Friday, Saturday & Sunday
- **Groups**
  By prior arrangement only

Features:
- *Restaurant*

Wines: Total wine production of up to 480,000 bottles a year
Wine sales at Visitors' Centre, at selected local & national stockists & online

Winemaker: Jonathan Medard

SPARKLING

Classic Cuvée – 2018
- 12.5% – *Classic Method*
- Brut – *(5.0 g/lt) – Creamy & yeasty aromas/lemon curd & apple pie*
- Pinot Noir *(57%)*, Chardonnay *(22%)*, Pinot Meunier *(21%)*

Blanc de Blancs – 2018
- 12.5% – *Classic Method*
- Brut – *(4.0 g/lt) – Lemon curd & croissant/fresh grapefruit & peach*
- Chardonnay *(100%)*

Blanc de Noirs – 2018
- 12.5% – *Classic Method*
- Brut – *(3.0 g/lt) – Baked apple & Morello cherries/plum compote*
- Pinot Noir *(93%)*, Pinot Meunier *(7%)*

Rosé – 2018
- 12.5% – *Classic Method*
- Brut – *(4.0 g/lt) – Cranberries, redcurrants & wineberries/quince*
- Pinot Noir *(63%)*, Chardonnay *(19%)*, Pinot Meunier *(18%)*

TILLINGHAM WINES (BIODYNAMIC)
(East Sussex)

Ben Walgate
Dew Farm, Dew Lane, Peasemarsh, TN31 6XD
info@tillingham.com
www.tillingham.com

11 en-suite bedroom converted Hop Barn (bed & breakfast)
Glamping facilities

This vineyard, overlooking the Tillingham River and Romney Salt marshes, within an area of rolling hills and near to the Cinque port of Rye, benefits from its own microclimate, has an unusual, and almost unique, selection of vines. It forms part of a 70 acre mixed use farm that dates back to the 13th century. The mixed use includes fruit trees, livestock and natural ancient woodland. This present vineyard owner, together with the land owner Viscount Devonport, has planted 21 varietals of vine in total at this location. Within the vinification process some of the grapes are foot trodden and a number of the wines are unfiltered with both oak and stainless steel storage being used. Another form of storage is the Georgian Qvevri, a form of amphora. The existing farm buildings have been modified, converted and restored to fulfil the requirements of this very modern vineyard which has produced up to 22 different vintages and styles of wine.

Vineyard:
- 20.00 acres under vine
- Between 0 & 40m. above sea level
- Mainly south facing slopes
- Clay soils on sandstone
- First vines planted in 2018
- Approximately 2,000 vines to the acre

Winery:
- Sparkling wine – White
- Still wines – White, Rosé & Red

Cider Press:

Visitors' Centre:
- **Open:**
  All year round:
  Wednesday to Sunday (09.00 to 17.00)
- **Guided tour & tasting:**
  By appointment only
- **Groups by prior arrangement only**

Features:
- Restaurant

Wines: Total wine production of around 50,000 bottles a year
Wine sales at Visitors' Centre, at selected local stockists & online

Winemaker: Ben Walgate

SPARKLING

Traditional Method – 2018
- 12.5% – *Classic Method*
- Brut – *(<1.0 g/lt) – BBrioche & melon/saline citrus & round palate*
- Pinot Noir *(50%)*, Pinot Blanc *(50%)*

WHITE

Qvevri White – 2021
- 10.0% – *Smokey, chalky melon & peach/stone fruit & earthy minerality*
- Bacchus, Pinot Blanc

Endgrain – 2021
- 10.0% – *Elderflower, citrus & white peach/spicey notes & salinity*
- Bacchus, Madeleine Angevine, Ortega, Muller-Thurgau

Field Blend One – 2021
- 10.5% – *Baked apple & honey notes/complex crisp salinity*
- 10 varieties (6 white, 4 red)

Field Blend Two – 2021
- 10.1% – *Jasmine, beeswax & quince/crisp citrus greengage & spice*
- 5 varieties (2 white, 3 red)

Pinot Blanc – NV
- 10.79% – *peach & wet rocks/green hazelnut & stone fruit*
- Pinot Blanc

Flor – NV
- 10.47% – *Tangerine & manzanilla sherry/bright acidity & oa*
- Chardonnay

ROSÉ

Rosé – 2021
- *10.5% – rosé petals & cardamon/crunchy cranberry*
- Pinot Noir, Pinot Blanc

RED

R – 2022
- 9.64% – *Red berries & flowers/juicy mouthfeel*
- Regent

Pinot Noir – 2021
- % – *Raspberry & spice/sweetness & light tannin*
- Pinot Noir

TILLINGHAM WINES (BIODYNAMIC) (KENT)

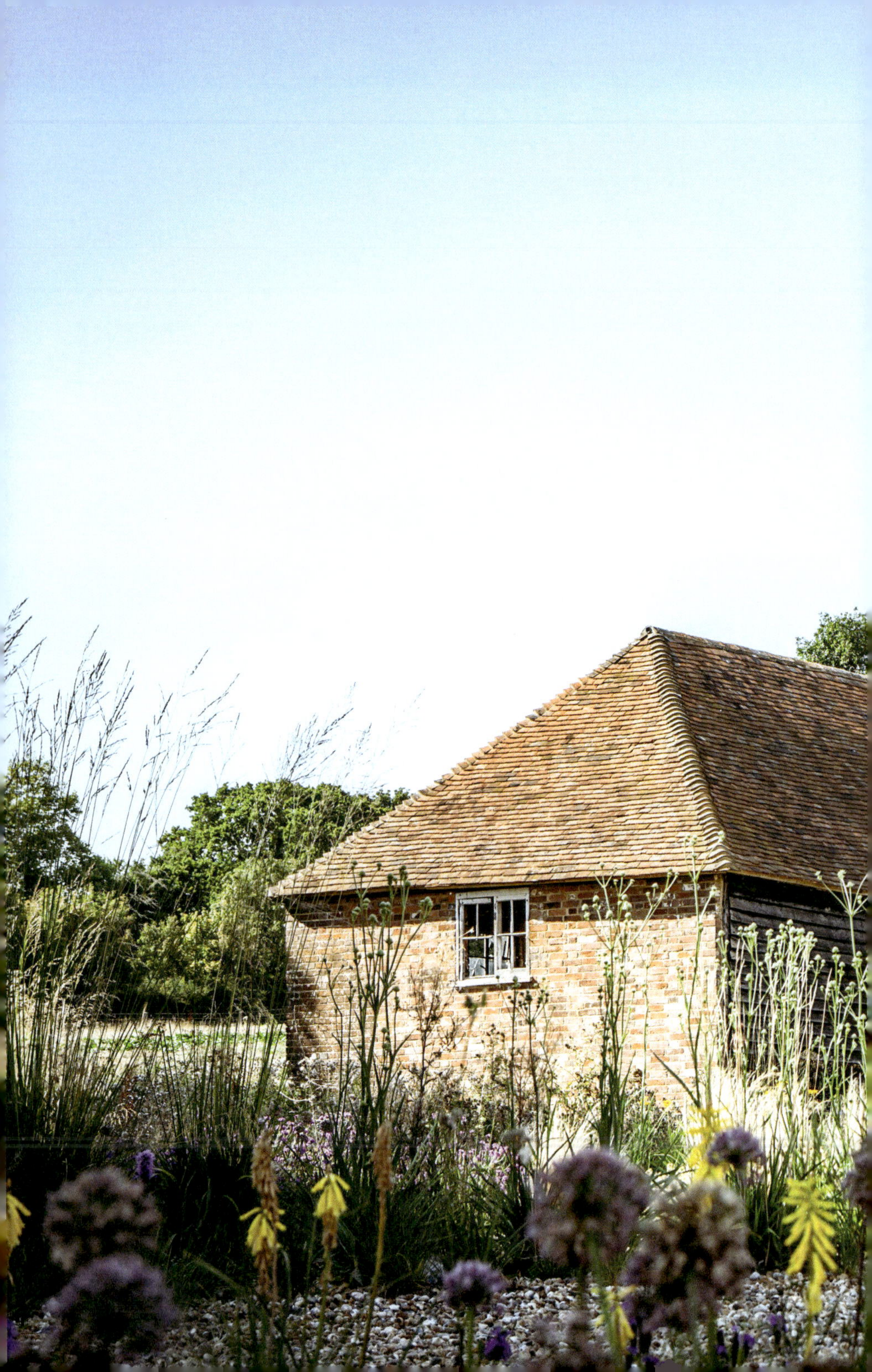

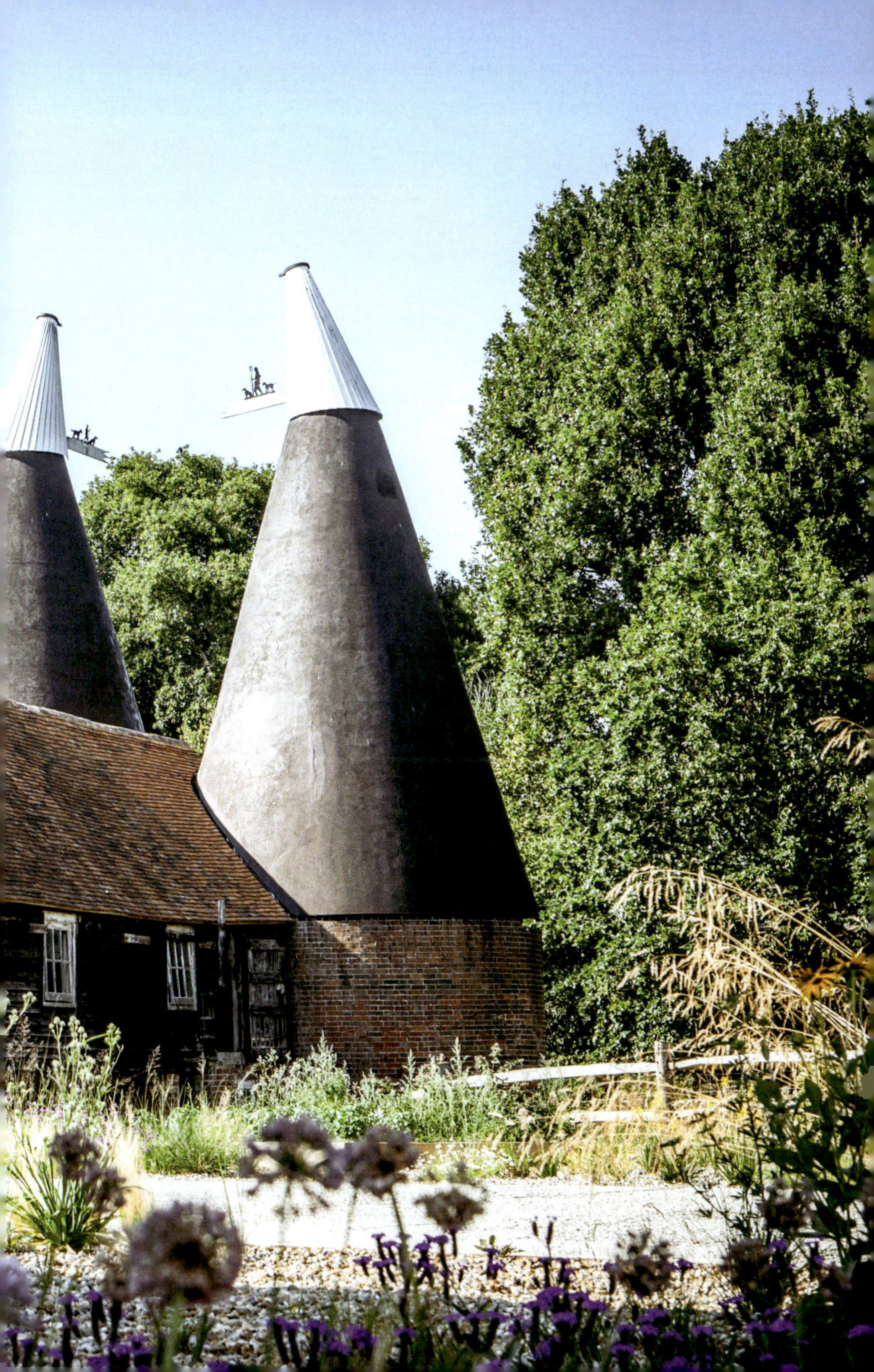

TERLINGHAM VINEYARD
(Kent)

The Wilks Family
Terlingham Lane, off Gibraltar Lane,
Hawkinge, CT18 7AE   01303 892452
contact@terlinghamvineyard.co.uk
www.terlinghamvineyard.co.uk

3 en-suite bedrooms (bed & breakfast)

These present owners bought this existing vineyard, which is only 10 minutes from Folkestone, on the Kent North Downs, and with a view of the English Channel, that had been planted by the previous owners on their family farm, in 2011. What started off as a couple's newly found lifestyle experience has now become a whole family operation. Methods have changed with time when, in 2015, these owners decided to adopt 'Natural farming' methods that involve an eco-friendly and sustainable approach. All activities have no intervention and processes are undertaken manually to make this a sustainable vineyard venture.

Vineyard:

- 4.0 acres under vine
- Between
- South facing slope
- Chalky soil
- First vines planted in 2006
- Approximately 1,250 vines to the acre

- Sparkling wines – White & Rosé
- Still wines – White, Rosé & Red

Vineyard Shop:

- **Open:**
  By appointment only
- **Guided tour & tasting:**
  Thursday & Saturday
  By appointment only

Features:

- Function facilities

Wines: Total wine production of between 2,000 & 4,000 bottles a year
         Wine sale at Vineyard Shop & online

Winemaker: Nick Lane (at Defined Wines)

SPARKLING

Sparkling White – 2019
- % – *Classic Method*
- Brut – *(g/lt) –*
-

Sparkling Rosé – 2020
- 11.0% – *Classic Method*
- Extra Brut – *(g/lt) – Orchard fruit & pie crust/ripe lemon & blossom fruit*
- Chardonnay *(%)*, Pinot Noir *(%)*, Pinot Meunier *(%)*

WHITE

Chardonnay – 2021
- 12.5% – *Lemon & green peach/ sweet orchard fruits*
- Chardonnay

ROSÉ

Pinot Noir & Dornfelder – 2021
- % – *Wild raspberry, ginger & blackcurrant/red apple, thyme & cherry plum*
- Pinot Noir, Dornfelder

RED

Caesar's Camp – 2018
- 10.0% – *Dense bramble/ blackcurrant, clove, spice &liquorice*
- Rondo, Dornfelder

TERLINGHAM VINEYARD (KENT)

EAST ANGLIA AND EAST MIDLANDS

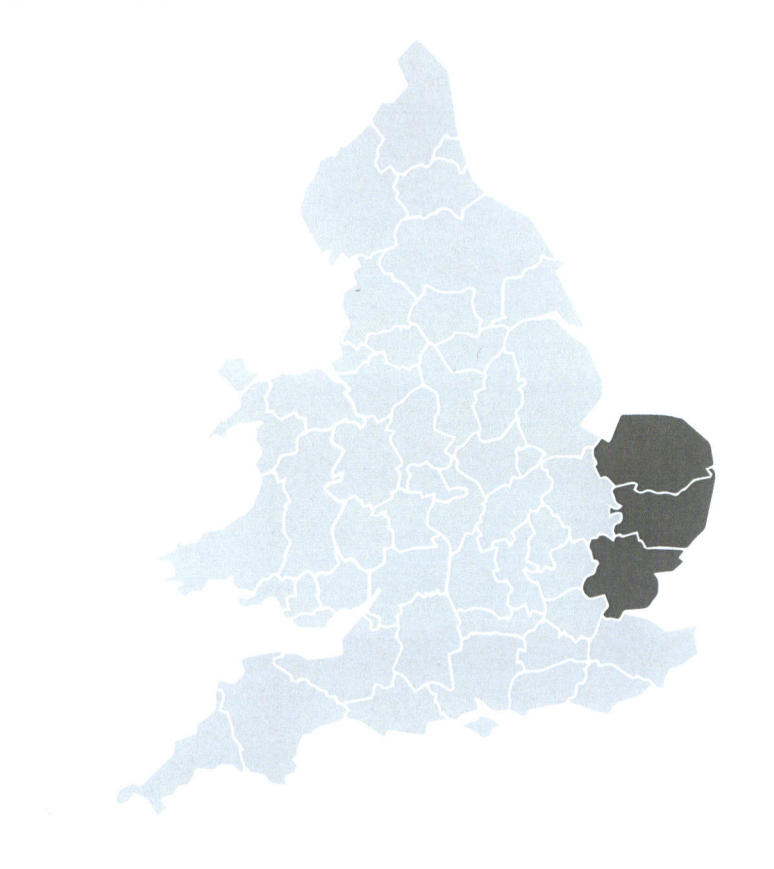

ESSEX

Bardfield Vineyard (Organic) 98

Crouch Ridge Vineyard 100

Mersea Island Vineyard 104

Toppesfield Vineyard 106

SUFFOLK

Valley Farm Vineyard 108

NORFOLK

Chet Valley Vineyard 110

BARDFIELD VINEYARD (ORGANIC)
(Essex)

Rebecca Jordan
Great Lodge, Great Bardfield, Braintree,
CM7 4QD   01371 810776
info@greatlodge.co.uk
www.greatlodge.co.uk

1 x 1 bedroom converted Barn (self-catering)
1 x 2 bedroom converted Barn (self-catering)
1 x 3 bedroom converted Barn (self-catering)

The vineyard, and farm, forms a very small acreage in the Great Lodge Estate. This Estate covers almost 1,000 acres of arable farm and woodland. Originally known as Great Park, an enclosed park owned by the Crown, initially by Elizabeth de Burgh, and used for hunting Fallow Deer, up to 1550. The deer, together with some Alpacas, still roam the Estate. The Grade I listed brick and tile 'Anne of Cleeves' barn dates from that same period when it is believed she lived at the adjacent Hall, Great Lodge, which is situated in the nearby village, after her marriage to Henry VIII had been annulled. The land and buildings, that form the farm have had many owners since that time until the present owners' family eventually bought it in 1951 after farming there since the early 1900's. Unfortunately many of the older farm buildings were demolished in the 1950s due to the cost of maintenance. Rosemary Alexander, of the London Physic Garden, was the owner for a number of the years in the 1980s and 1990s. A certain amount of replanting was carried out in 2015 and 2016, by the present owner, and the vineyard part of the farm has been managed organically since 2017.

Vineyard:

- 2.00 acres under vine
- Around 76m. above sea level
- North/South facing slope
- Chalky boulder clay soil
- First vines planted in 1989
- Approximately 1,150 vines to the acre

- Sparkling wine – White
- Still wines – White

Cellar Door:

- **Open:**
  All year round:
  Weekdays (10.00 to 16.00)
- **Guided tour & tasting:**
  May to September:
  1st Thursday of each month (11.30)
- **Self-guided walkabout**
  When open

Features:

- *Function facilities*
- *Licensed for civil ceremonies*

Wines: Total wine production of around 6,000 bottles a year
              Wines sales at Cellar Door & online

Winemaker: Steve Gillham (at New Hall vineyard)

SPARKLING

Brut – 2018 ⭘
- 🛢 12.0% – *Classic Method*
- 🍷 Brut – *(g/lt) – Pear & ripe apricots/ crisp apple & floral notes*
- 🍇 Pinot Noir *(46%)*, Bacchus *(38%)*, Seyval Blanc *(16%)*

WHITE

Bacchus – 2021 ⭘
- 🍷 11.0% – *Aromas of elderflower & grapefruit/herbaceous notes & fruity apple*
- 🍇 Bacchus

Anne of Cleeves – 2019 ⭘
- 🍷 11.0% – *Elderflower & grapefruit/ herbaceous notes, apple & medium dry finish*
- 🍇 Bacchus

BARDFIELD VINEYARD (ORGANIC) (ESSEX)

CROUCH RIDGE VINEYARD
(Essex)

Ross & Samantha Lonergan
Althorne Hall Farm, Fambridge Road,
Althorne, CM3 6BZ   07970 527892
info@crouchridge.com
www.crouchridge.com

6 x 2 bedroom luxury Apartments (self-catering)
1 x 5 bedroom luxury converted Barn (self-catering)

Overlooking the Althorpe Creek and the River Crouch this vineyard has been planted, within the existing farm, by the 5th generation of the Essex family that had toiled this land which has been, up to now, dairy then beef then arable. At the edge of the farm on the banks of the river there was once an Oyster Shack selling oysters directly from the river estuary. Due to this nearness to the water, its regional meteorological location, and together with the protection of recently planted woodland, the vineyard benefits from its own micro-climate. The first planting was of 2.5 acres with the vineyard gradually being enlarged to its present size over the years. With the failure of the first planting some replacement planting of unresponsive root stock took place in 2012.

Vineyard:

- *15.00 acres under vine*
- *Around 47m. above sea level*
- *Gentle south facing slopes*
- *Clay soil with mineral deposits*
- *First vines planted in 2010*
- *Approximately 1,250 vines to the acre*

- *Sparkling wines – White & Rosé*
- *Still wines – White, Rosé & Red*

Cellar Door:

- **Open:**
  All year round:
  Wednesday to Sunday (10.00 to 18.00);
  Other times: By appointment only
- **Guided tour & tasting:**
  Easter to September:
  Various Saturdays
  By appointment only
- **Groups:**
  By prior arrangement only

Features:

- *Seasonal events*
- *Restaurant*
- *Function facilities*
- *Disability access*

Wines: Total wine production of up to 25,000 bottles a year
           Wine sales at Cellar Door & online

Winemaker: Steve Gillham (at New Hall vineyard) & John Worontschak
           (at Litmus Wine)

SPARKLING

Premier Cuvée Brut – 2018
- 12.5% – *Classic Method*
- Brut – *(<1.0 g/lt) – Peach, white flowers & vanilla pod/fresh fruit, brioche & honey*
- Chardonnay *(60%)*, Pinot Noir *(40%)*

Blanc de Blancs – 2018 ()
- 12.5% – *Classic Method*
- Brut – *(<1.0 g/lt) – Lemon sherbet & elderflower/apple, lemon & peach*
- Chardonnay *(100%)*

Pinot Rosé Reserve – 2020
- 12.5% – *Classic Method*
- Brut – *(<1.0 g/lt) – Floral & vanilla/brioche & lemon*
- Pinot Noir *(100%)*

WHITE

Reserve Chardonnay – 2021
- 12.0% – *Pear & red fruit aromas/red fruit, pear & strawberry*
- Chardonnay

Single Estate Bacchus – 2021
- 11.0% – *Aromatic grapefruit & pear/peaches & lime*
- Bacchus

ROSÉ

Pinot Noir Rosé – 2021 ()
- 11.5% – *Summer fruit aromas/minerality & red fruit flavours*
- Pinot Noir

RED

Pinot Noir Reserve – 2020
- 13.0% – *Light bodied red berries & plum/red fruit, earthy spices & silky tannins*
- Pinot Noir

CROUCH RIDGE VINEYARD (ESSEX)

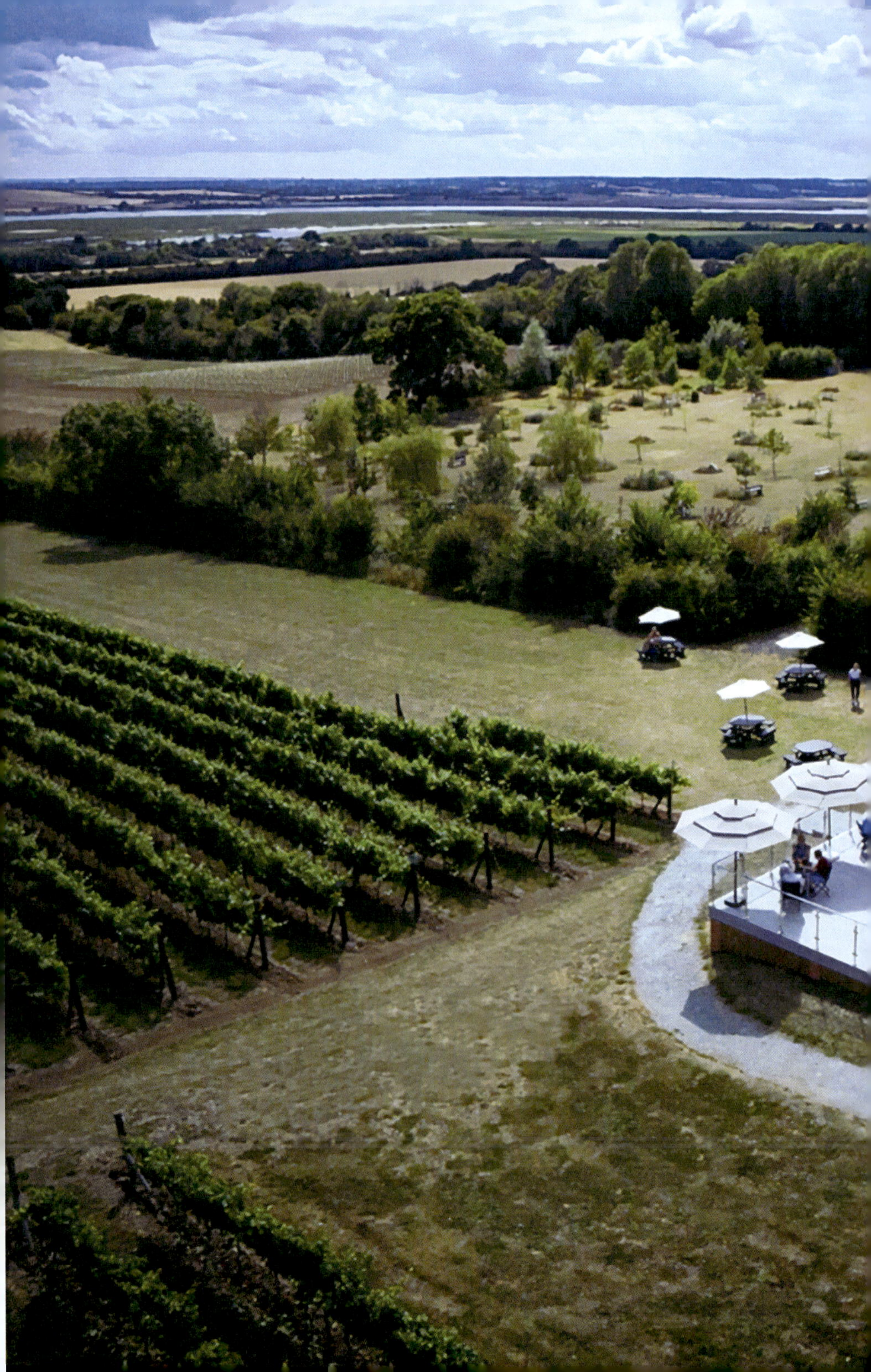

CROUCH RIDGE ESTATE

MERSEA ISLAND VINEYARD
(Essex)

Roger Barber
Rewsalls Lane, East Mersea, Colchester,
CM5 8SX   01206 385900
mark@merseabrewery.com
www.merseaislandvineyard.co.uk

5 en-suite holiday bedrooms (bed & breakfast)

On a site, believed to have been a Roman vineyard, between the estuaries of the Blackwater and Colne rivers, just south of Colchester, is this present day vineyard. It is reached by a tidal causeway that is subject to flooding with the Spring tides. Because of the island situation it benefits from a particular micro-climate. These present owners bought this existing vineyard in 1997 and expanded its then size with some new planting and have also extensively modernised the vineyard and its facilities.

Vineyard:
- 10.00 acres under vine
- Between 1 & 8m. above sea level
- South facing site
- Mainly clay soil
- First vines planted in 1985
- Approximately 1,000 vines to the acre

- Still wines – White & Rosé

Distillery:
- Gin

Brewery:
- Craft ales

Visitors' Centre:
- **Open:**
Easter to October:
Thursday to Sunday (10.00 to 16.00)
Monday to Wednesday:
By appointment only

Features:
- Tea Room
- Function facilities
- Licensed for civil ceremonies

Wines: Total wine production of around 20,000 bottles a year
Wine sales at Visitors' Centre, at selected local stockists & online

Winemaker: Steve Gillam (at New Hall vineyard)

WHITE	ROSÉ
Island Dry – NV	**Blush – NV**
🍷 11.0% – *Crisp & fresh/slight acidity*	🍷 11.0% – *Summer fruit flavours*
🍇 Reichensteiner	🍇 Muller-Thurgau, Pinot Noir
Mehala – NV	
🍷 11.0% – *Aromatic/citrus & elderflower flavours*	
🍇 Ortega	
Summer Days – NV	
🍷 11.0% – *Medium dry*	
🍇 Muller-Thurgau	

MERSEA ISLAND VINEYARD (ESSEX)

TOPPESFIELD VINEYARD
(Essex)

Jane & Peter Moore
Bradfields, Harrow Hill, Toppesfield,
CO9 4LX   01787 237228
info@toppesfieldvineyard.co.uk
www.toppesfieldvineyard.co.uk

1 x 2 en-suite bedroom luxury Villa (self-catering)

The present owners bought this late 14th century house in 2000 to take their professional careers into the countryside. The house had been the home of Michael Ayrton, the artist, writer and sculpture, and the existing barn had been his studio. However when some agricultural land, adjacent to the house, became available in 2011 they bought it and decided to indulge their passion for English wine and plant a vineyard. Roman remains had been found on the land in the 1800's indicating that there had probably been a vineyard in the vicinity in that era. The vineyard, as well as benefitting from suitable soils and orientation, has the benefit of a particularly suitable micro-climate with this part of the country being probably the driest in the UK. With the vineyard being basically a weekend activity it is to some extent dependant upon the local community. This community was voted 'Essex Village of the Year' in 2016 for its total enterprise and commitment.

Vineyard:

- 3.0 acres under vine
- Around 60m. above sea level
- Westerly facing slope
- Clay loam soil over fertile chalk
- First vines planted in 2012
- Approximately 2,000 vines to the acre

- Sparkling wines – White & Rosé
- Still wines – White & Rosé

Wine Centre:

- **Open:**
  For the benefit of residents
- **Tour & tasting:**
  For the benefit of residents

Features:

- Cultural events
- Function facilities

Wines: Total wine production of around 8,000 bottles a year
Wine sales at Wine Centre, at selected local stockists & online

Winemaker: Steve Gillham (at New Hall vineyard)

SPARKLING

Classic – 2018
- 12.5% – *Classic Method*
- Brut – *(6.5 g/lt) – Crisp apple &red berry/tiny well formed bubbles*
- Pinot Noir *(72%)*, Chardonnay *(28%)*

Rosé – 2018
- 12.5% – *Classic Method*
- Brut – *(2.1 g/lt) – Summer berries/ creaminess & tiny well formed bubbles*
- Pinot Noir *(100%)*

WHITE

Bacchus Reserve – 2021 ()
- 11.0% – *Dry & fruity/gooseberry, nettle & elderflower*
- Bacchus

ROSÉ

Pinot Rosé – 2021 ()
- 11.0% – *Strawberries & citrus/ refreshing finish*
- Pinot Noir Precoce

TOPPESFIELD VINEYARD (ESSEX)

VALLEY FARM VINEYARD
(Suffolk)

Adrian Cox
The Vinery, Rumburgh Road, Wissett,
IP19 0JJ   07867 009967
info@valleyfarmvineyards.co.uk
www.valleyfarmvineyards.co.uk

1 x 2 person Eco Cabin (self-catering)

First planted by Jonathan Craft within a 14 acre site, the vineyard, known as Wissett Wine at that time, had been expanded up to its full size by 1992. It was then bought by Vanessa Tucker & Elaine Heeler as a complete change in lifestyle for them in 2014. They then undertook a four-year programme of the restoration and renovation of the original rootstock and brought the acreage down to its present size. In 2021 the vineyard was bought by the present owner and his son. They are looking to further modernise and extend both the vineyard and its facilities. The vineyard lies in a shallow valley a few miles inland from the Suffolk Heritage coast and is sheltered from the easterly winds by a bank of Italian Alder hedges.

Vineyard:

- 8.00 acres under vine
- Between 25 & 35m. above sea level
- South facing slope
- Flinty alluvial soils
- First vines planted in 1987
- Approximately 375 vines to the acre

- Sparkling wine – White
- Still wines – White & Rosé

Cellar Door:

- **Open:**
  All year round:
  Wednesday to Friday (10.00 to 17.00);
  Saturday & Sunday (12.00 to 16.00)
- **Guided tour & tasting:**
  April to October:
  1st Saturday in the month
- **Self-guided walkabout:**
  When open

Wines: Total wine production of around 10,000 bottles a year
            Wine sales at Cellar Door, by mail order & online

Winemaker: David Brocklehurst (at Knightor Winery)

SPARKLING

Sundancer – 2013
- 13.0% – *Classic Method*
- Brut – *(g/lt) – Baked apple, patisserie, almonds & honey/lemon & shortbread*
- Pinot Noir *(1/3)*, Pinot Meunier *(1/3)*, Auxerrois *(1/3)*

WHITE

Madeleine Angevine – 2019
- 11.5% – *Stone fruit, apple & hedgerow flowers/citrus & ripe cox apple*
- Madeleine Angevine

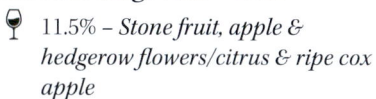

Pinot Gris – 2019
- 11.0% – *Pear, honeysuckle & jasmine/peach, grapefruit & steely acidity*
- Pinot Gris

ROSÉ

View East – 2020
- 11.0% – *Strawberry, cherry, candid sweets & hantilly cream/citrussy clean & crisp finish*
- Madeleine Angevine, Pinot Noir

VALLEY FARM VINEYARD (SUFFOLK)

CHET VALLEY VINEYARD
Part of **Proudly Norfolk** (Norfolk)

John Hemmant
Loddon Road, Berg Apton, NR15 1BT
01508 333002
info@chetvineyard.co.uk
www.chetvineyard.co.uk

1 x 3 bedroom holiday Cottage (self-catering)

The vineyard, on the edge of the Fens and open to the coast to the east, forms a small part of a much larger general purpose farm that has been in the present family since the early 1900's. It is now in the ownership of the 4th generation of the family and it is this generation that has planted the vineyard. The ground, having been well trodden by horses, together with the local climate, is well suited to the growing of vines. With having a scientific background the owner has a particular approach to the winemaking in the on site winery that was built in 2020.

Vineyard:
- *20.00 acres under vine*
- *Between 40 & 49m. above sea level*
- *Undulating south facing*
- *Sandy loam & gravel over boulder clay*
- *First vines planted in 2010*
- *Approximately 1,200 vines to the acre*

Winery:
- *Sparkling wines – White & Rosé*
- *Still wines – White, Rosé & Red*

Cellar Door:
- **Open:**
  April to October:
  Monday to Friday (10.00 to 16.50);
  Saturday (10.00 to 18.00)
  Other times:
  By appointment only
- **Guided tour & tasting:**
  April to October:
  Wednesday (11.00) &
  Saturday (11.00 & 15.00)
- **Self-guided walkabout:**
  When open
- **Groups:**
  By prior arrangement only

Wines: Total wine production of around 8,000 bottles a year
Wine sales at Cellar Door, at local stockists & online

Winemaker: John Hemmant

SPARKLING

Skylark – 2021 ()
- 12.0% – *Classic Method*
- Brut – *(9.0 g/lt) – Apple, lime & white peach/apricot, pear & tropical fruit*
- Phoenix *(%)*, Seyval Blanc *(%)*

Skylark – 2021
- 12.0% – *Classic Method*
- Demi-Sec – *(22.0 g/lt) – Aromatic apple & white peach/apricot & tropical fruit*
- Phoenix *(80%)*, Seyval Blanc *(15%)*

Blanc de Blancs – 2020
- 12.0% – *Classic Method*
- Brut – *(g/lt) – Dry & linear/apple, pear & citrus*
- Chardonnay *(100%)*

Blanc de Noirs –
- % – *Classic Method*
- Brut – *g/lt) – Red apple & strawberry/brioche*
- Pinot Noir *(68%)*, Pinot Meunier *(32%)*

Red Kite – 2021 ()
- 12.0% – *Classic Method*
- Brut – *(9.0 g/lt) – Cranberry & cherry aromas/light tannins & good length*
- Regent *(100%)*

WHITE

Swift – 2022 ()
- ( )% – *Lemon, quince & rosé petal/elderflower & lychee*
- Schonburger

Siskin – 2022
- 11.0% – *Fruity & yeasty//apple, pear, lemon & melon*
- Solaris

Stonechat – 2022
- % – *Gooseberry, citrus & spice*
- Sauvignon Blanc

ROSÉ

Redwing – 2022 ()
- 11.0% – *Apple, citrus & hazelnut/herbaceous honey notes*
- Pinot Noir, Regent

RED

Robin Redbreast – 2022
- ( )% – *Red berry characteristics*
- Cabernet Noir

CHET VALLEY VINEYARD (NORFOLK) 111

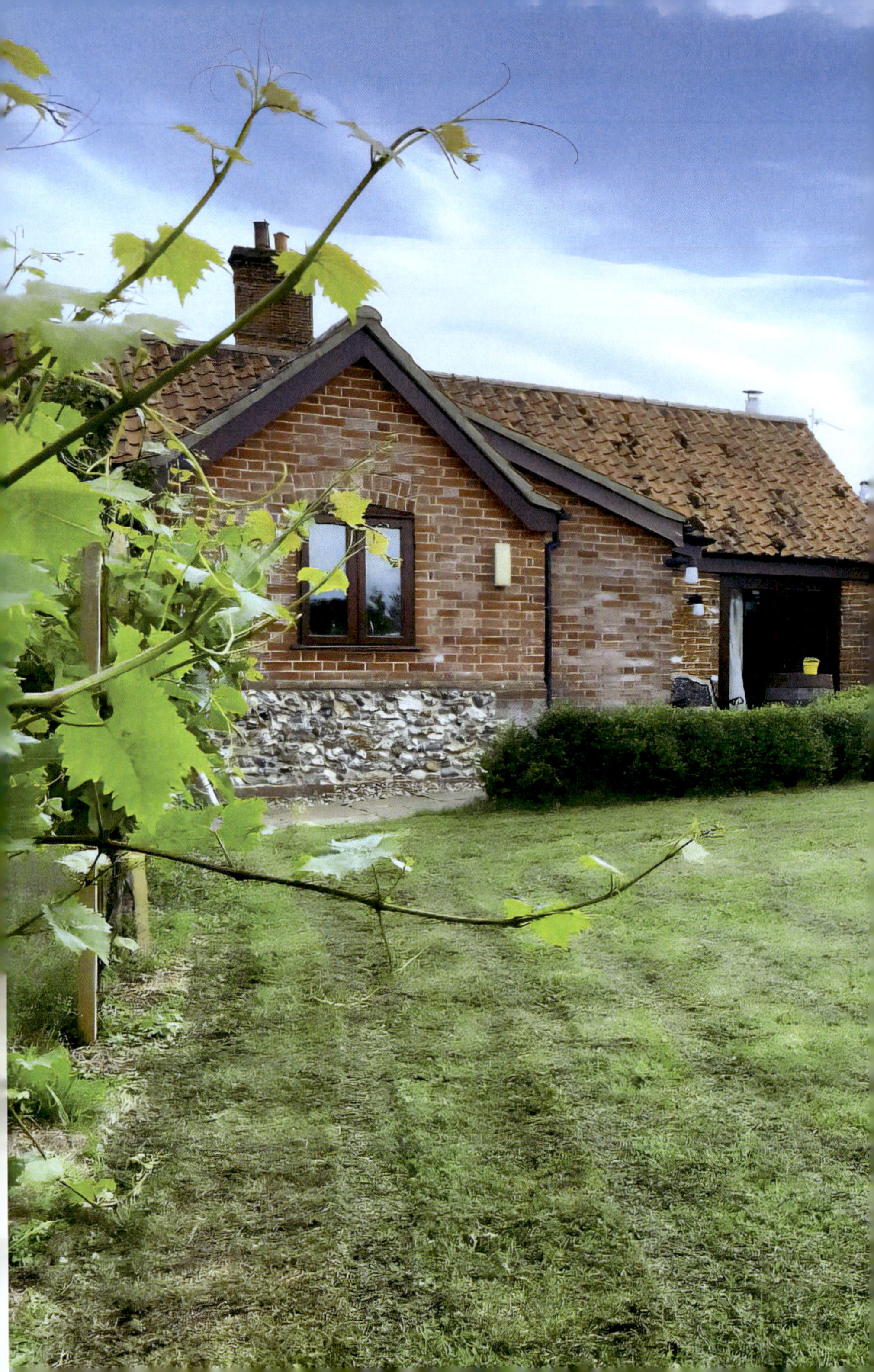

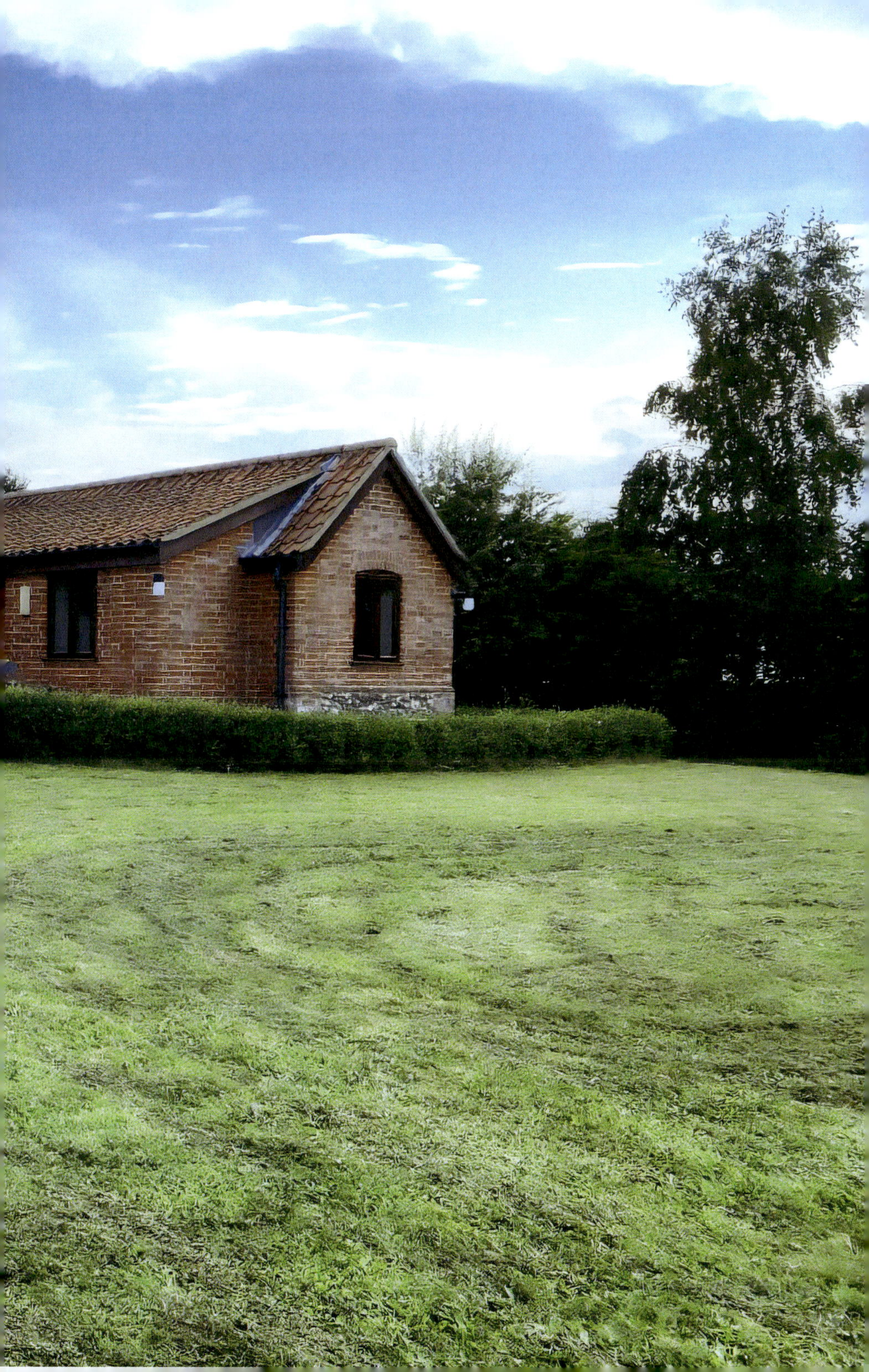

WEST MIDLANDS AND SOUTH WALES

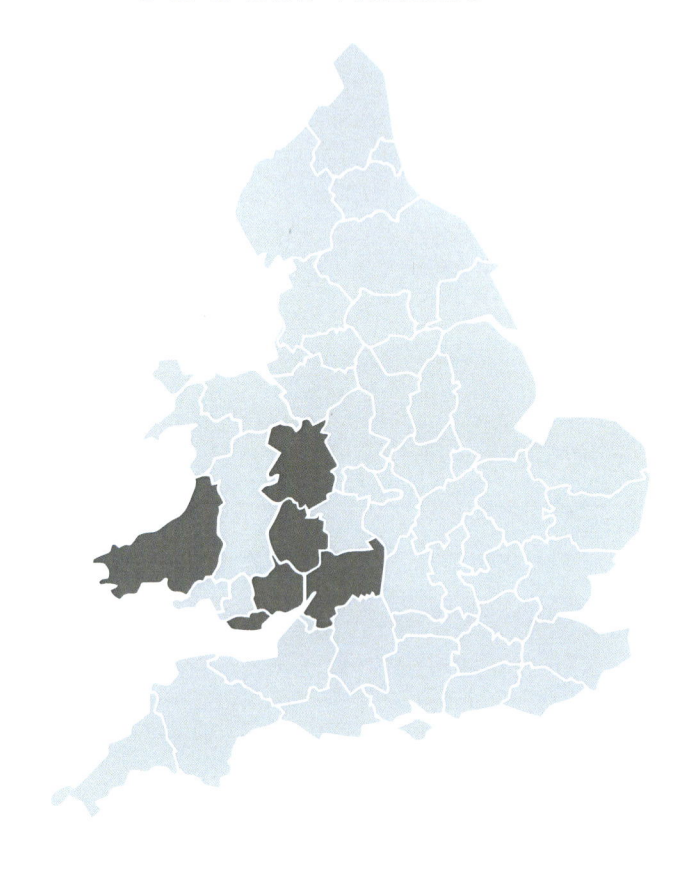

GLOUCESTERSHIRE

Poulton Hill Estate Vineyard   116

Three Choirs Vineyard   118

Woodchester Valley Vineyard   122

HEREFORDSHIRE

Coddington Vineyard   124

Wythall Estate Vineyard   126

VALE OF GLAMORGAN

Glyndwr Vineyard   128

Llanerch Vineyard   130

CARMARTHENSHIRE

Jabajak Vineyard   134

SHROPSHIRE

Hencote Vineyard   136

POULTON HILL ESTATE VINEYARD
(Gloucestershire)

Caroline Findlay
Poulton, Down Ampney, GL7 5JA
01285 850257
contact@poultonhillestate.co.uk
www.poultonhillestate.co.uk

3 en-suite bedroom converted Barn (bed & breakfast)

A flock of rare breed Old English Babydoll Southdown sheep forage between the vines keeping the grass down at the same time as fertilizing the soil. The vineyard is a family run enterprise that is situated in the heart of the Cotswold Water Park, an area where there is a 2000 year history of wine making. It is situated at the junction of three Roman roads, the Fosse Way, Akeman Street and Ermin Street, and near to Cirencester, that had been known as Corinium, the second largest town in Roman Britain, and capital of Britannia Prima. The vineyard was voted 'Best Vineyard in the Cotswolds' for 2020.

Vineyard:
- 8.50 acres under vine
- Around m. above sea level
- South facing slopes
- soil
- First vines planted in 2010
- Approximately 1,100 vines to the acre

- Sparkling wines – White & Rosé
- Still wines – White, Rosé & Red

Distillery:
- Brandy

Cellar Door:
- **Open:**
  June to October:
  Monday to Friday;
  Selected Saturdays
- **Guided tour & tasting:**
  June to October:
  Occasional Monday to Friday (11.0);
  Selected Saturdays (11.0)

Wines: Total wine production of around 20,000 bottles a year
Wine sales at Cellar Door, at selected local & national stockists & online

Winemaker: Martin Fowke (at Three Choirs vineyard)

SPARKLING

Bulari – 2018 ()
- 11.5% – *Classic Method*
- Brut – *(g/lt) – Green apple, orange peel & lime/grapefruit & lemon*
- Seyval Blanc *(65%)*, Pinot Noir *(35%)*

Bulari Rosé – 2018 ()
- 11.3% – *Classic Method*
- Brut – *(g/lt) – Passion fruit & hints of orange/crisp, dry finish*
- Seyval Blanc *(65%)*, Rondo *(35%)*

WHITE

Special Reserve – 2021 ()
- 11.0% – *Elderflower & pear/peach, zesty lemon & sherbet*
- Seyval Blanc, Phoenix

Bacchus – 2021 ()
- 11.5% – *Elderflower & ripe peach/grapefruit & lychee*
- Bacchus

Phoenix – 2021 ()
- 11.5% – *Elderberry, herbaceous hints/lychee & gooseberry*
- Phoenix, Seyval Blanc

Arlington White – 2020 ()
- 10.5% – *Elderflower & gooseberry/passion fruit, lime & honey*
- Phoenix, Seyval Blanc, Bacchus

ROSÉ

Rosé – 2021
- 11.0% – *Strawberry & delicate rosé/summer fruits & long finish*
- Seyval Blanc, Bacchus, Phoenix, Rondo

Pinot Noir Rosé – 2020
- 11.3% – *Cherries & strawberry/summer berries*
- Pinot Noir

RED

Arlington Red – NV ()
- 12.0% – *Cherry, blackberry & strawberry hints/red berries, damson & hints of raspberry*
- Rondo, Regent

POULTON HILL ESTATE VINEYARD (GLOUCESTERSHIRE)

THREE CHOIRS VINEYARD
(Gloucestershire)

Thomas Shaw
Baldwins Farm, Newent, GL18 1LS
01531 890223
info@threechoirs.com
www.three-choirs-vineyards.co.uk

8 en-suite Bedrooms (bed & breakfast)
3 x 2 person luxury vineyard Lodges (bed & breakfast)

The vineyard is situated close to the Welsh border, in an area of natural beauty, and benefits from its own particular micro-climate being on the edge of the Vale of Evesham. The first vines, on just half an acre, were planted as an experiment within his 100 acre fruit farm by Alan McKecknie. In 1984 he wanted to sell. A group of local businessmen and vineyard owners bought the farm and started a new enterprise. This was under the leadership of John Oldacre and involved providing co-operative facilities for these vineyard owners and others around. At this time the name was changed from Fairfield Fruit Farms to Three Choirs Vineyard. 1990 saw the building of the winery and this was followed in 2000 and 2008 by the various holiday accommodation. The vineyard has grown over the years and has now developed into one of the larger single site vineyards in the UK. As a part of this development has been the need to replace some of the vines due to their age. The vineyard produces a 'First Release' on the third Thursday in November to rival 'Beaujolais Nouveau' although this one is white.

Vineyard:
- 75.00 acres under vine
- Between 24 & 70m. above sea level
- South & south-west facing slopes
- Well drained sandstone soils
- First vines planted in 1974
- Approximately 800 vines to the acre

Winery:
- Sparkling wines – White & Rosé
- Still wines – White, Rosé & Red

Visitors' Centre:
- **Open:**
  All year round:
  Daily (09.00 to 17.00)
- **Guided tour & tasting:**
  Saturday & Sunday (11.30 & 14.00)
  By appointment only
- **Groups by prior arrangement only:**
  Max 6 persons

Wines: Total wine production of around 250,000 bottles a year
Wine sales at Visitors' Centre, by mail order, at selected local & national stockists & online

Winemaker: Martin Fowke

SPARKLING

Classic Cuvée – NV ⭕
- 🛢 11.8% – *Classic Method*
- 🍷 Brut – *(7.2 g/lt) – Green apple & stone fruits/biscuit & brioche*
- 🍇 Seyval Blanc, Pinot Noir, Phoenix

Blanc de Noirs – 2014 ⭕
- 🛢 11.7% – *Classic Method*
- 🍷 Brut – *(8.2 g/lt) – Citrus hints/ classic biscuit & brioche*
- 🍇 Pinot Noir *(100%)*

Pinot Noir Rosé – 2017
- 🛢 12.0% – *Classic Method*
- 🍷 Brut – *(12.3 g/lt) – Soft summer fruits/classic biscuit & brioche*
- 🍇 Pinot Noir *(100%)*

WHITE

May Hill – 2021
- 🍷 10.6% – *Grapefruit/ripe citrus fruits & honey*
- 🍇 Reichensteiner, Phoenix, Huxelrebe, Solaris, Orion

Bacchus – 2021 ⭕
- 🍷 11.83% – *Nettle & elderflower hints/ crisp citrus & zesty finish*
- 🍇 Bacchus, Orion

Siegerrebe – 2021
- 🍷 11.0% – *Aromatic spice/lychee & grapefruit*
- 🍇 Siegerrebe

Coleridge Hill – 2021
- 🍷 11.1% – *Hedgerow aromas & crisp apple/ripe fruit & balanced acidity*
- 🍇 Phoenix, Madeleine Angevine, Seyval Blanc, Orion

First Release – 2022
- 🍷 11.5% – *Fresh fruit salad/peach & lychee*
- 🍇 Solaris, Muller-Thurgau, Siegrrebe, Bacchus

ROSÉ

Rosé – 2021
- 🍷 11.27% – *Subtle berry fruit aromas/ crisp fresh finish*
- 🍇 Phoenix, Seyval Blanc, Madeleine Angevine, Pinot Noir, Triomphe, Others

RED

Pinot Noir – 2018 ⭕
- 🍷 11.55% – *Rich strawberry aromas/ subtle farmyard notes*
- 🍇 Pinot Noir Precoce

Ravens Hill – 2020
- 🍷 12.0% – *Blackberry & cherry/red berry fruit*
- 🍇 Regent, Rondo, Triomphe, Others

THREE CHOIRS VINEYARD (GLOUCESTERSHIRE)

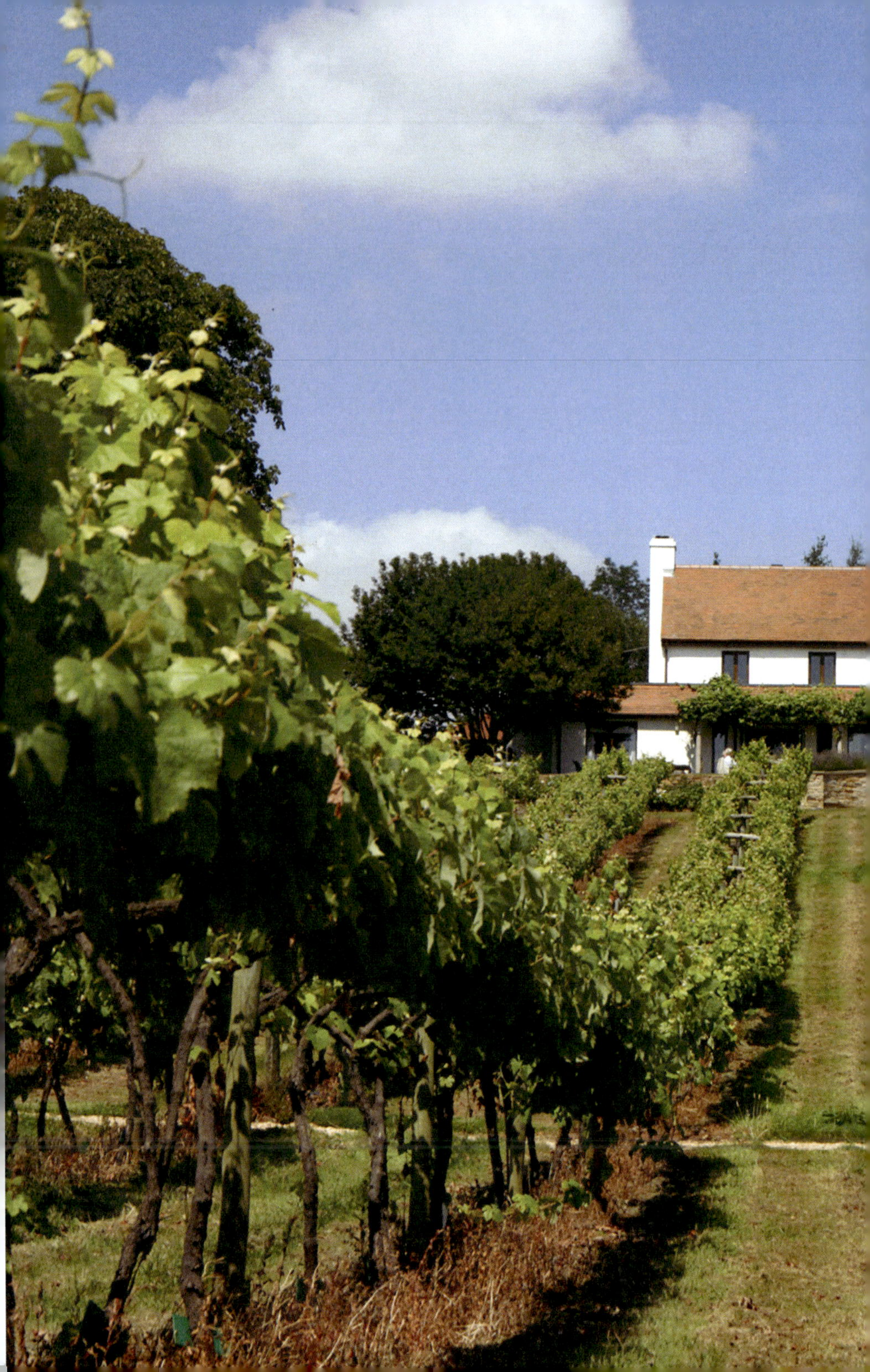

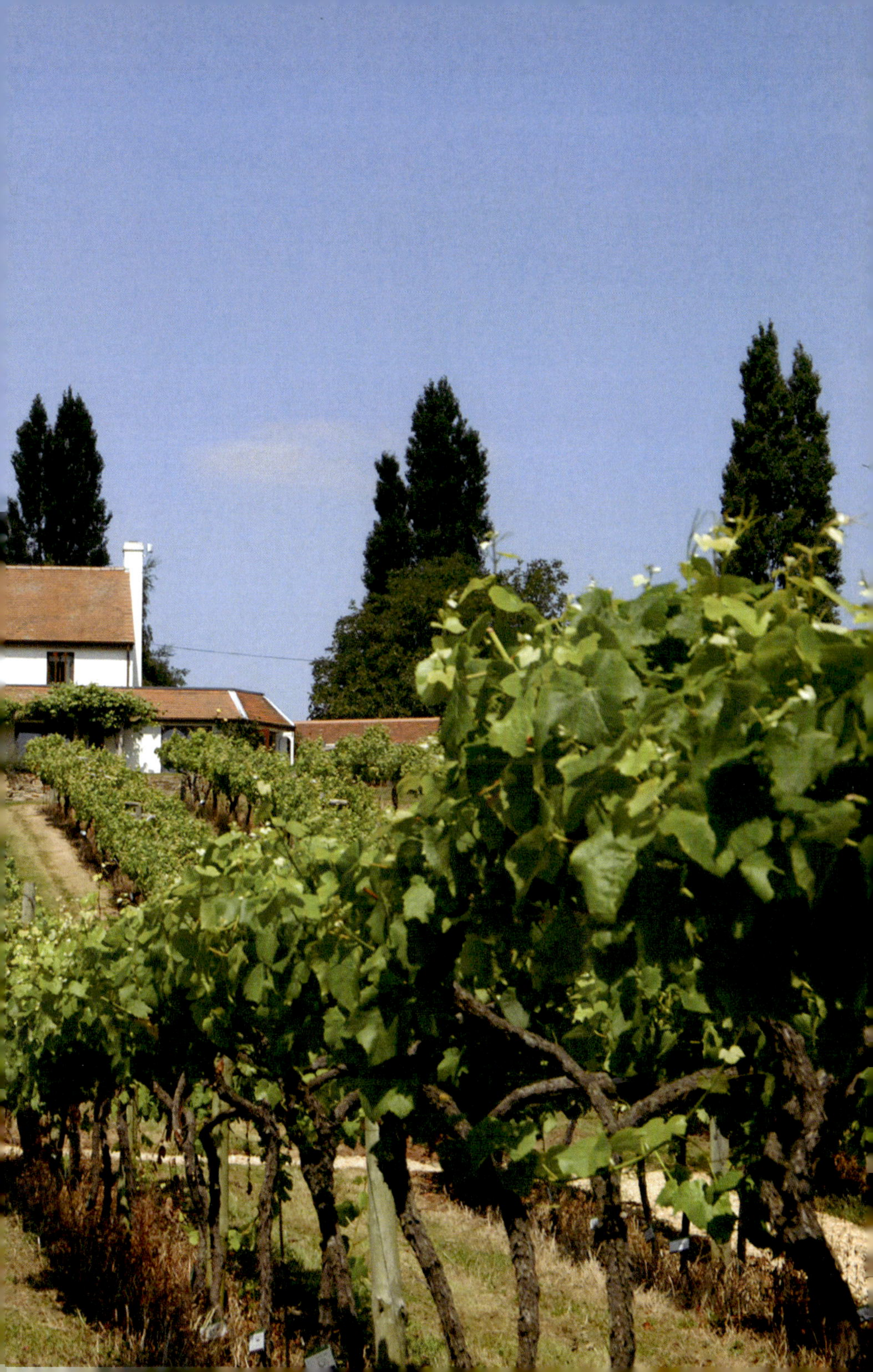

WOODCHESTER VALLEY VINEYARD
(Gloucestershire)

Fiona Shiner
Culver Hill, Amberley, GL5 5BA
07523 967219
info@woodchestervalleyvineyard.co.uk
www.woodchestervalleyvineyard.co.uk

3 luxury guest Bedrooms (bed & breakfast)
1 x 2 bedroom Farmhouse (self-catering)
1 x 6 bedroom Valley House (self-catering)

Sitting at the edge of the Cotswold escarpment within the South Cotswolds Area of Outstanding Natural Beauty the vineyard forms one of three sites under the same ownership. The present owners made the initial planting of 1 acre as an experiment to find out about the suitability of the soils. The initial planting was so successful that it created a change for lifestyle for the owners and further plantings were carried out in 2011, 2012, 2013, 2015 and 2019. These plantings were all within the Stroud Valleys and are in an area where the Doomsday Book of 1086 mentioned the location of two vineyards. The vineyard is family run and the in-house winery, built in 2016, made the total enterprise self-sufficient. The Orpheus Roman pavement of 200/400 AD is within the vicinity although not open to the public.

Vineyard:
- 55 acres under vine
- Between 60 & 150m. above sea level
- South, east & south-west facing slopes
- Cotswold brash over Oolitic limestone
- First vines planted in 2007
- Approximately 1,800 vines to the acre

Winery:
- Sparkling wines – White & Rosé
- Still wines – White, Rosé & Red

Cellar Door:
- **Open:**
  All year round:
- *Monday to Saturday (10.00 to 18.00)*
- **Guided tour & tasting:**
  All year round:
  Tuesday to Sunday (various times & tours)
  By appointment only

Wines: Total wine production of between 60,000 & 120,000 bottles a year
Wine sales at Cellar Door & online

Winemaker: Jeremy Mount

SPARKLING

Cotswold Classic – 2019 ◯
- 12.0% – *Classic Method*
- Brut – *(12.5 g/lt) – Fresh orchard fruit & wildflowers/gentle toasty notes*
- Seyval Blanc *(75%)*, Pinot Blanc *(25%)*

Reserve Cuvée – NV ◯
- 12.0% – *Classic Method*
- Brut – *(9.0 g/lt) – Complex/ripe red fruit & subtle red apple*
- Pinot Noir, Chardonnay, Pinot Meunier

Blanc de Blancs – 2017
- 12.0% – *Classic Method*
- Brut – *(g/lt) – Baked apple, citrus & biscuit/buttery nectarines*
- Chardonnay *(100%)*

Rosé Brut – 2019 ◯
- 12.5% – *Classic Method*
- Brut – *(9.0 g/lt) – Ripe raspberries & toasted aromas/delicate bubbles*
- Pinot Noir *(82%)*, Pinot Meunier *(18%)*

WHITE

Bacchus – 2021 ◯
- 11.5% – *Elderflower, zesty citrus & gooseberry/lychee aromas & flavours*
- Bacchus

Culver Hill – 2021 ◯
- 12.0% – *Citrus & green fruits/peach & hints of minerality*
- Ortega, Bacchus, Seyval Blanc

Orpheus Bacchus – 2021
- 12.0% – *intergrated elderflower & lychee/defined minerality & length*
- Bacchus

Ortega – 2021
- 11.5% – *Candied orange peel, roasted pears & apricot/vanilla & cinnamon*
- Ortega

ROSÉ

Rosé – 2021
- 11.5% – *Cranberries & raspberries/ ripe red fruits*
- Regent

Pinot Rosé – 2022
- % – *Red fruit aromas*
- Pinot Noir Precoce

RED

Atcombe Red – 2020 ◯
- 12.0% – *Red fruits & blueberries/ sweet black cherry & berry*
- Pinot Noir Precoce, Regent

WOODCHESTER VALLEY VINEYARD (GLOUCESTERSHIRE)

CODDINGTON VINEYARD
(Herefordshire)

Denis Savage
Coddington, HR8 1JJ
01531 641817
denis@coddingtonvineyard.co.uk
www.coddingtonvineyard.co.uk

1 x Grade II listed 2 bedroom Cottage (self-catering)
1 x 1 bedroom Log Cabin (self-catering)

This vineyard provided a change of direction for the owners from practising paediatrics to becoming a vineyard owner and winemaker. It is situated on a valley side where the local frosts roll down to the valley floor and is at the foot of the Malvern Hills in an area of Outstanding Natural Beauty. The vineyard is also probably one of the most picturesque in the UK, set within six acres of landscaped grounds. It was planted in what had been the farm orchard. All the vineyard equipment and facilities are housed is converted and re-used original farm buildings, the shop in the old apple Press House and the winery in an old barn, that all date back to previous centuries including the 18th. Local buzzards help to keep the vineyard free of starlings and other lovers of vines and grapes.

Vineyard:
- *2.00 acres under vine*
- *Between 73 & 91m. above sea level*
- *South facing slopes*
- *Clay loam soil over sandstone*
- *First vines planted in 1985*
- *Approximately 1,200 vines to the acre*

Winery:
- *Sparkling wine – White*
- *Still wine – White*

Cellar Door:
- **Open:**
  All year round:
  Friday & Saturday (10.00 to 16.00)
  Other times:
  By appointment only
- **Guided tour & tasting:**
  April to August:
  Occasional Saturdays (12.00)
- **Groups:**
  By prior arrangement only

Features:
- *Function facilities*
- *Licensed for civil ceremonies*

Wines: Total wine production of around 3,500 bottles a year
Wine sales at Cellar Door & online

Winemaker: Denis Savage

SPARKLING

Pinot Gris – 2019
- 12.5% – *Classic Method*
- Brut – *(g/lt) – Fine aromas/lively fruity zest & spicy flavours*
- Pinot Gris *(100%)*

WHITE

Bacchus – 2019 ◯
- 12.0% – *Hints of elderflower, nettle & rosé flower/tropical fruit flavours*
- Bacchus

Ortega – 2021
- 11.5% – *Peach, apple blossom & honeysuckle/zesty citrus, lime & passion fruit*
- Ortega

Oyster Hill – 2020
- % – *Aromatic*
- Pinot Gris, Ortega

CODDINGTON VINEYARD (HEREFORDSHIRE)

WYTHALL ESTATE VINEYARD
(Herefordshire)

Jamie McIntyre
Bulls Hill, Walford, Ross-on-Wye
HR9 5SD   01989 566868
info@wythallestate.co.uk
www.wythallestate.co.uk

1 x 1 bedroom Apartment (self-catering)
1 x 2 bedroom Apartment (self-catering)

The vineyard forms part of a Manorial Estate which dates back to the 16th century. Situated in the Wye Valley not far from Ross-on-Wye it benefits from the unique microclimate that is created by the surrounding undulating terrain and the stream at the foot of the vineyard. Planted within a small area of the Estate the vines are in widely spaced rows. The visitor facilities are to be found in converted service rooms of the original half-timbered Manor House, with the wine tastings taking place in the Hall's dining room. There are also open gardens and walks, together with a large lake, within the Estate.

Vineyard:

- 3.50 acres under vine
- Around 80m. above sea level
- Southerly facing slope
- Sandy loam soil
- First vines planted in 2010
- Approximately 1,000 vines to the acre

- Sparkling wines – White & Rosé
- Still wines – White & Red

Open:ing Times

- **Open:**
  February to December
  By appointment only
- **Guided tour & tasting:**
  Selected Saturdays (12.00)
  By appointment only
- **Groups:**
  By prior arrangement only

Wines: Total wine production of around 3,000 bottles a year
Wine sales at Manor House, at selected local stockists & online

Winemaker: Martin Fowke (at Three Choirs vineyard)

SPARKLING	WHITE

Special Reserve – 2015 ()
- 11.5% – *Classic Method*
- Brut – *(g/lt) – Fresh pears & baked apples/soft gentle mousse*
- Orion *(100%)*

Rosé – 2018 ()
- 11.5% – *Classic Method*
- Brut – *(g/lt) – Redcurrants & rosé water/red fruits, strawberries & dry finish*
- Orion (%), Rondo (%)

Siegerrebe – NV ()
- 11.5% – *White currants & nettle/fresh melon & ripe acidity*
- Siegerrebe

RED

Estate Red – NV ()
- 11.5% – *Plum & hint of cinnamon/red cherries, violets & liquorice*
- Rondo

Pinot Noir – NV ()
- 11.5% – *Black cherry & fesh raspberry/touch of earthiness & velvety finish*
- Fruhburgunder

WYTHALL ESTATE VINEYARD (HEREFORDSHIRE)

GLYNDWR VINEYARD
Vale of Glamorgan

Richard Norris
Llanblethian, Cowbridge, CF71 7JF
01446 774564
info@glyndwrvineyard.co.uk
www.glyndwrvineyard.co.uk

2 x 1 self-contained Studios (self-catering)

This vineyard is the oldest, largest and had probably been the first commercial one in Wales. Named after the Welsh national hero of the Middle Ages it is to be found within an area of rolling hills, and just four miles from the sea. It benefits from its own south Wales micro-climate, which is helped by the vineyard being enclosed by apple and pear trees. The area also benefits from a very high level of sunshine. The first planting was of three acres in an area adjacent to the owner's house and initiated a complete change of lifestyle for them. The house also accommodates the vineyard's wine store in its cellars. A steady increase of planting, over the years, has brought the vineyard up to its present size. It is now run jointly by two generations of the family. The grounds to the owner's house, and their adjoining orchard, are landscaped and open to the public on occasions as part of the National Garden Scheme.

Vineyard:
- 6.00 acres under vine
- Between 73 & 76m. above sea level
- South east facing slopes
- Light clay soils over limestone
- First vines planted in 1979
- Approximately 1,000 vines to the acre

- Sparkling wines – White & Rosé
- Still wines – White, Rosé & Red

Distillery:
- Brandy

Visitors' Centre:
- **Open:**
  April to October:
  Daily on request
- **Guided tours:**
  By appointment only

Features:
- Cider Press
- Function facilities
- Licensed for civil ceremonies

Wines: Total wine production of around 12,000 bottles a year
Wine sales at Visitors' Centre, at selected local & regional stockists & online

Winemaker: Martin Fowke (at Three Choirs vineyard)

SPARKLING

Vintage White – 2018 ◯
- 12.0% – *Classic Method*
- Brut – *(g/lt) – Full bodied & toasty/ripe fruit & fine bubbles*
- Seyval Blanc *(100%)*

Vintage Rosé – 2020
- 11.5% – *Classic Method*
- Brut – *(g/lt) – Delicate, light & crisp/mellowing orchard fruit*
- Triomphe *(%)*, Seyval Blanc *(%)*

WHITE

Dry White – 2022
- 11.0% – *Spring flowers, apple & peach/herbaceous & long finish*
- Reichensteiner, Seyval Blanc

ROSÉ

Rosé – 2021
- 11.0% – *Freshly cut hay*
- Triomphe, Seyval Blanc

RED

Red – 2021
- 12.0% – *Berry & savoury nuances/complex & fruity*
- Rondo

GLYNDWR VINEYARD (VALE OF GLAMORGAN)

LLANERCH VINEYARD
Vale of Glamorgan

Ryan Davies
Hensol Road, Hensol, Pendoylan
CF72 8GG   01443 222716
info@llanerch.co.uk
www.llanerch-vineyard.co.uk

37 en-suite bedroom Luxury Hotel (bed & breakfast)
1 x 2 person holiday Apartment (self-catering)
Cottages (self-catering)

The vineyard was planted some years after the original owners, Peter and Diana Andrews, purchased the former 20 acre dairy farm in the late 1970's to create a family home. The farm, and many of its buildings, dates back to the 1700's. They were inspired by the fact that an ancient vineyard to Cardiff Castle had been only a short distance away and that vines had been planted in this area of Wales in Victorian times. These later vines had been grubbed up by the end of the first World War. The Andrews planted their first vines, in what had been a paddock adjacent to the house, in 1986, thus creating one of the oldest modern day vineyards in Wales. There was a change of ownership in 2007. However when the present owner bought the vineyard in 2010 he was the youngest vineyard owner in the UK. The vineyard, at that time, appeared to have been neglected for two years. Since the purchase he has restored the old original farm buildings and replaced a number of the old vines. Further planting has taken place in the last year. The planting is in unusually wide single and double rows and is planted North/South on the gentle slope. Within the confines of the vineyard there is a 10 acre area of mature woodland and a three acre natural lake.

Vineyard:

- 13.00 acres under vine
- Between 55 & 61m. above sea level
- South facing slopes
- Sand loam soils
- First vines planted in 1986
- Approximately 1,250 vines to the acre

- Sparkling wines – White & Rosé
- Still wines – White & Rosé

Features:

- Cookery School
- Restaurant
- Function facilities
- Licensed for civil ceremonies

Visitors' Centre:

- **Open:**
  All year round:
  Monday to Saturday (10.00 to 23.00;
  Sunday (12.00 to 23.00)
- **Guided tour & tasting:**
  Daily (13.30, 15.00 & 17.00)
- **Self-guided walkabout:**
  When open
- **Groups:**
  By prior arrangement only

Wines: Total wine production of around 12,000 bottles a year
Wine sales in House

Winemaker: Martin Fowke (at Three Choirs vineyard)

SPARKLING

Cariad White – 2016
- 11.5% – *Classic Method*
- Brut – *(g/lt) – Bright fruit aromas/ rich characteristics & smooth effervescence*
- Seyval Blanc *(100%)*

Cariad Blush – 2016
- 11.5% – *Classic Method*
- Brut – *(g/lt) – Summer berry fruit/ juicy crisp citrus fruit & delicate mousse*
- Seyval Blanc *(95%)*, Triomphe *(5%)*

WHITE

Dry – NV
- 10.0-11.0% – *Lively citrus & green fruit/crisp refreshing finish*
- Solaris, Phoenix

Poplar – NV
- 10.0-11.0% – *Light & aromatic/ripe fruit flavours & elderflower notes*
- Reichensteiner, Solaris

ROSÉ

Blush – 2020
- 10.0-11.0% – *Raspberry & strawberry/refreshingly slight sweetness*
- Reichensteiner, Madeleine Angevine, Triomphe

LLANERCH VINEYARD (VALE OF GLAMORGAN)

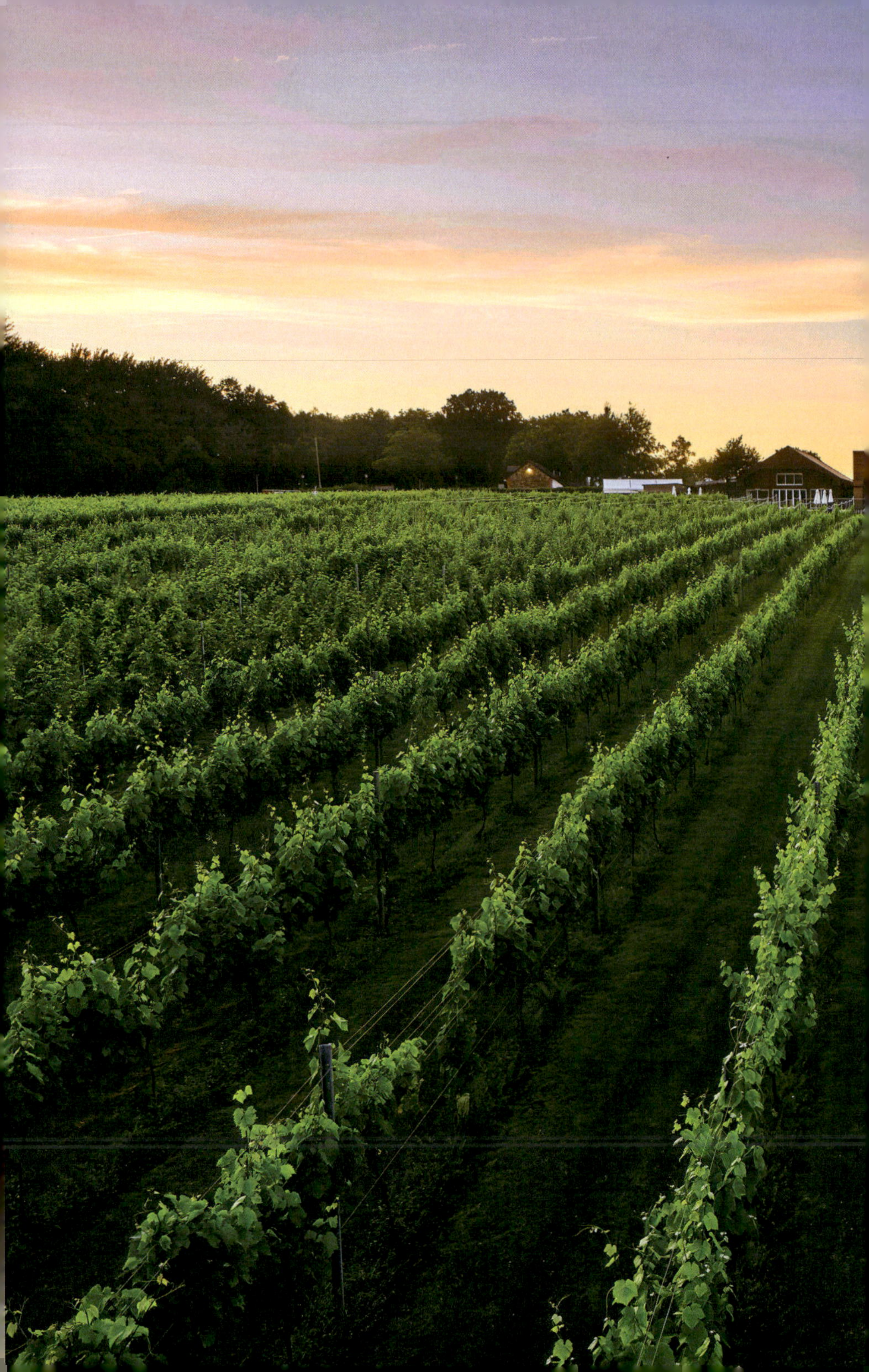

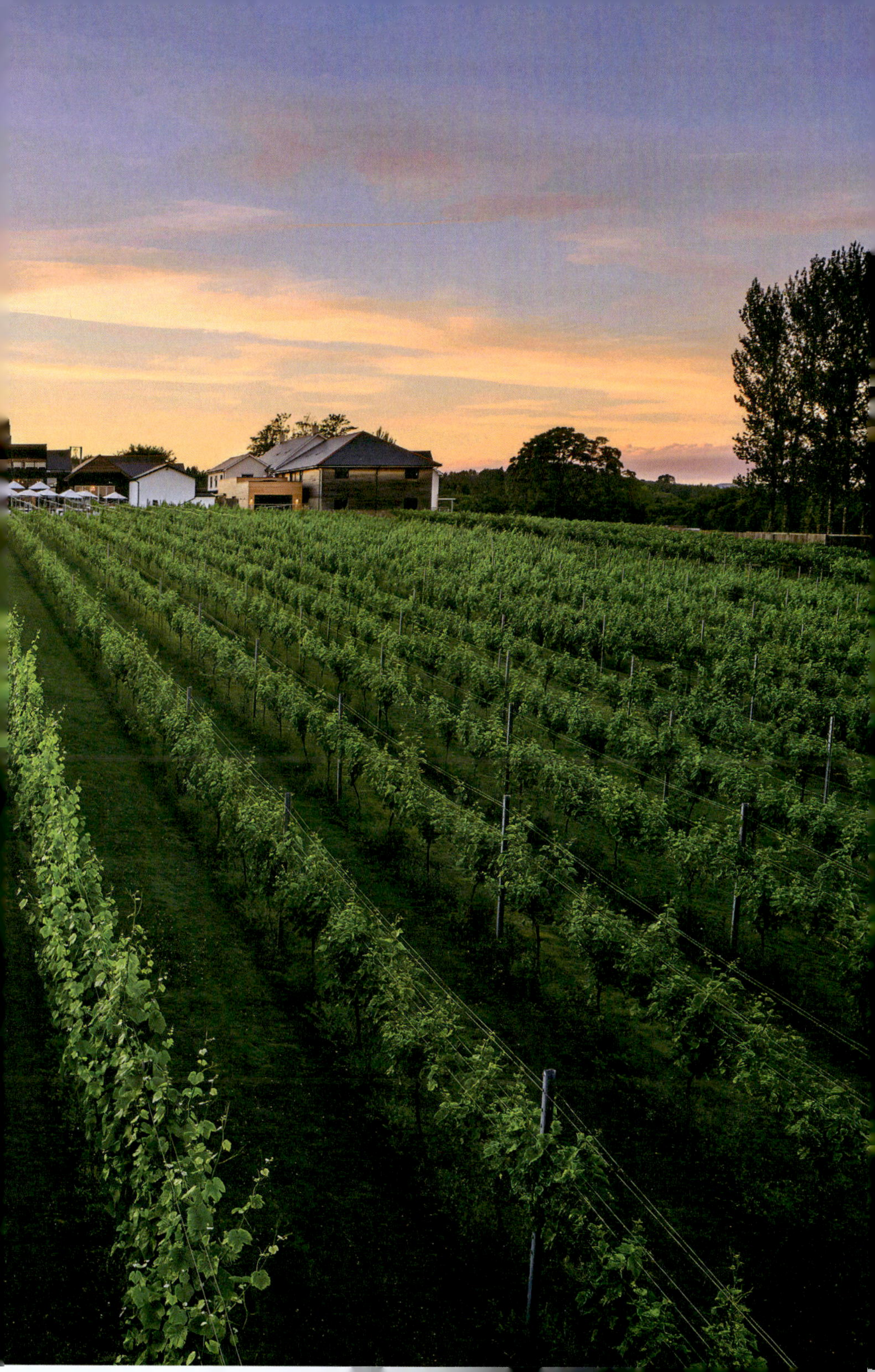

JABAJAK VINEYARD
(Carmarthenshire)

Julian & Amanda Stuart-Robson
Blanc-y-Llain, Llanboidy Road,
Whitland, SA34 0ED
01994 448786
info@jabajak.co.uk
www.jabajak.co.uk

4 en-suite Annex bed-rooms (bed & breakfast)
1 x 2 person en-suite Farmhouse bedroom (bed & breakfast)
1 x 2 person Farmhouse suite (bed & breakfast)
2 x 2 person private suites (bed & breakfast)

What started off as a restoration and conversion project of a run-down, 19th-century smallholding in 1998, for the present owners, it soon progressed into something more ambitious. This involved the restoration of the existing farm house and the building of hospitality facilities. Then came the vineyard which from planting took around five years to produce their first acceptable grapes. The seven acres of the estate sit on the borders of three counties, Pembroke, Carmarthan and Ceredigan, in the heart of West Wales on the edge of the Bluestone mountain range and contains an abundance of wild life. It is a registered feeding point for the local red kites. The estate, in which the vineyard is planted, is home to 'The White House' which is featured on the label of the bottles of wine, and has a historical connection with that building bearing the same name in the U.S.A. An early tenant of the original farm was the grandfather of President John Adams the first occupant of that famous building.

Vineyard:
- 6.00 acres under vine
- Around m. above sea level
- South facing gentle slopes
- Red limestone soil over rocky slate
- First vines planted in 2007
- Approximately 800 vines to the acre

- Sparkling wine – White & Rosé
- Still wine – White & Red

Visitors' Centre:
- **Open:**
  All year round:
  Daily
- **Guided tour & tasting:**
  Daily (17.30)
  By appointment only
- **Self-guided walkabout:**
  When open after 14.30

Features:
- Restaurant
- Function facilities

Wines: Total wine production of around 3.000 bottles a year
Wine sales at Visitors' Centre & online

Winemaker: Martin Fowke (at Three Choirs vineyard)

SPARKLING	WHITE

White House – 2018
- ( )% – *Classic Method*
- Brut – *(g/lt)* –
- Seyval Blanc *(50%)*, Phoenix *(50%)*

White House – 2021
- ( )% – *Fresh fruity aromas/zesty palate & crisp finish*
- Seyval Blanc

Rosé Blush – 2016
- ( )% – *Classic Method*
- Brut – *(g/lt)* – *Strawberry aromas/ summer berries*
- Seyval Blanc *(49%)*, Phoenix *(49%)*, Rondo *(2%)*

RED

Red – 2018
- ( )% – *Fruit character/damson & cherry*
- Rondo

JABAJAK VINEYARD (CARMARTHENSHIRE)

HENCOTE VINEYARD
(Shropshire)

Mark Stevens
Cross Hill, Shrewsbury, SY4 3AA
01743 298444
reception@hencote.com
www.hencote.com

7 en-suite bedroom restored Georgian Hay Barn (self-catering)
10 x 2 person luxury Lodges (self-catering)

In 1997 the present owners moved in to this existing farm in order to make Hencote their family home after spending many years travelling the world. In 2009 a Dora Stevens planted a hobby vineyard of 200 vines which produced an almost undrinkable wine. However in 2015 after the family had undertaken a proper and thorough investigation of the land they decided to plant some 18,000 vines as the land had been determined as being suitable for the growing of grape vines. That number has now risen to a total of 23,000. The resulting vineyard, benefiting from its own particular local micro-climate and the Shropshire terroir, sits in the glacially formed rolling countryside on the banks of the River Severn with Wrekin hill, the Welsh hills and Shrewsbury beyond. A 200 year old Sycamore provides a feature of the landscape as well as a marketing emblem. Gradual development has seen the winery and additional facilities completed by 2019. The vineyard is a family affair with two generations totally involved.

Vineyard:
- 16.50 acres under vine
- Between 50 & 85m. above sea level
- South facing slope
- Glacial till soils over sandstone
- First vines planted in 2009
- Approximately 1,400 vines to the acre

Winery:
- Sparkling wine – White
- Still wine – White, Rosé & Red

Cellar Door:
- **Open:**
  May to September
- **Vineyard tour & tasting:**
  Thursday to Sunday (11.00 & 14.00)
- **Winery tour & tasting:**
  October to April:
  Thursday to Sunday (11.00 & 14.00)

Features:
- Bistro
- Restaurant
- Function facilities
- Licensed for civil ceremonies

Wines: Total wine production of around 30,000 bottles a year
Wine sales at Cellar Door & online

Winemaker: Gavin Patterson

SPARKLING

Evolution – 2020 ◯
- 10.9% – *Classic Method*
- Brut – *(9.39 g/lt) – Crabapple & hedgerow/scintillating freshness*
- Seyval Blanc *(53%)*, Pinot Noir *(31%)*, Solaris *(9%)*, Pinot Meunier *(7%)*

LXX – 2018
- 11.7% – *Classic Method*
- Brut – *(7.25 g/lt) – Complex refinement*
- Pinot Noir *(100%)*

Isadora – 2018
- 12.5% – *Classic Method*
- Brut – *(7.6 g/lt) – Summer berries & strawberries & cream*
- Pinot Meunier *(55%)*, Pinot Noir *(30%)*, Chardonnay *(15%)*

WHITE

Amphora Chardonnay – 2018 ◯
- 11.5% – *Bold, lifted & fresh/good depth of flavour*
- Chardonnay

Vivienne – 2021
- 12.75% – *Citrus & tropical notes/passion fruit, pineapple & crunchy fruit*
- Solaris, Chardonnay

ROSÉ

Suzanne – 2021
- 12.0% – *Fresh strawberries & sherbet/ripe fruit & long finish*
- Pinot Noir

RED

Mark III – 2021 ◯
- 12.0% – *Black cherry & cranberry/savoury palate*
- Pinot Noir, Pinot Noir Precoce, Rondo

Amphora Pinot Noir – 2018 ◯
- 11.5% – *Redcurrant, rosé hip & red cherry/firm long finish*
- Pinot Noir

HENCOTE VINEYARD (SHROPSHIRE)

NORTH WALES AND NORTH OF ENGLAND

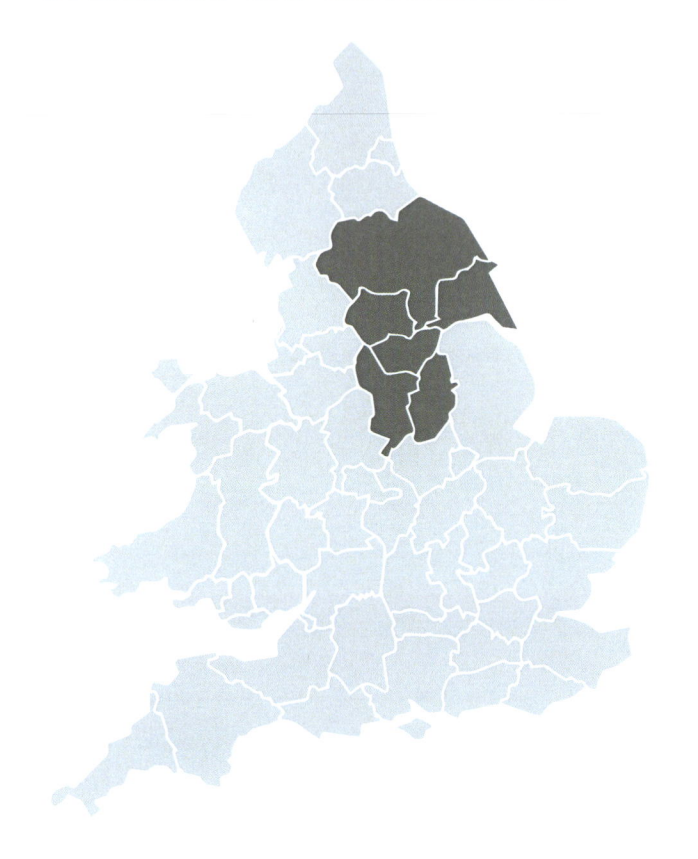

NOTTINGHAMSHIRE

Hanwell Wine Estate 140

DERBYSHIRE

Sealwood Cottage Vineyard 142

YORKSHIRE

Ryedale Vineyards 144

Sheveling Wine Estate 146

Yorkshire Heart Vineyard 148

HANWELL WINE ESTATE
(Nottinghamshire)

William & Helenka Brown
Melton Road, Hickling Pastures, Melton Mowbray, LE14 3QG
01949 81393
helenka.brown@hotmail.co.uk
www.hanwellwine.co.uk

Glamping facilities
Caravan Park

Tony Skuriat created his own 'Eglantine' vineyard and winery a short distance away in 1980. Now Helenka, his daughter, has planted her own vineyard as part of this 35 acre agricultural holding in South Nottinghamshire to be the second vineyard owner in the family. Since the initial planting the vineyard has seen a continual development of its facilities and services. Dad, of course, makes the wine.

Vineyard:

- *8.00 acres under vine*
- *Around 100m. above sea level*
- *South west facing slope*
- *Rich loam & clay soil*
- *First vines planted in 2012*
- *Approximately 1,000 vines to the acre*

- *Sparkling wine – White*
- *Still wines – White & Rosé*

Features:

- *Rural Craft Workshops*
- *Selected events*
- *Café*
- *Function facilities*

Cellar Door:

- **Open:**
  All year round:
  Saturday (13.00 to 16.00)
  May to September:
  Friday (10.00 to 16.00)

- **Guided tour & tasting:**
  March to September:
  Saturday (13.00) – Spring;
  Friday to Sunday (13.00) – Summer & Autumn

- **Self-guided walkabout:**
  When open

Wines: Total wine production of around 2,000 bottles a year
Wine sales at Cellar Door & online

Winemaker: Tony Skuriat (at Eglantine vineyard)

SPARKLING

Rainbow's Reward – 2016
- 12.5% – *Classic Method*
- Brut – *(4.0 g/lt) – Crisp & yeasty/ lemon notes & toasty finish*
- Pinot Noir *(60%)*, Pinot Meunier *(40%)*

Classic – 2017
- 12.5% – *Classic Method*
- Brut – *(g/lt) – Green apple & fresh lemon/lemon sherbet & biscuit*
- Chardonnay *(%)*, Pinot Noir *(%)*, Pinot Meunier *(%)*

Scarlet Cloak – 2017
- 12.5% – *Classic Method*
- Brut – *(g/lt) – Raspberries, redcurrants & cherries/freshly baked bread*
- Pinot Noir *(%)*, Pinot Meunier *(%)*

Sunset Sparklee – 2015
- % – *Classic Method*
- Brut – *(g/lt) – Lemon/yeasty edge*
- Chardonnay *(%)*, Pinot Noir *(%)*, Pinot Meunier *(%)*

Blush – 2018
- 12.5% – *Classic Method*
- Brut – *(g/lt) – Fresh summer berries/gala apples, white peach & shortcrust pastry*
- Chardonnay *(%)*, Pinot Noir *(%)*, Pinot Meunier *(%)*

WHITE

New Dawn – NV
- 11.0% – *Zesty citrus fruit flavours/ mellow finish*
- Chardonnay, Pinot Noir, Pinot Meunier

First Love – NV
- 11.0% – *Red apple aromas & palate/clean & fresh finish*
- Pinot Noir, Pinot Meunier

ROSÉ

Romance – NV
- 11.0% – *Red apple*
- Pinot Noir, Pinot Meunier

HANWELL WINE ESTATE (NOTTINGHAMSHIRE)

SEALWOOD COTTAGE VINEYARD
(Derbyshire)

John & Elizabeth Goodall
Sealwood Lane, Linton, Swadlincote,
DE12 6PA   01283 761371
vineyard@sealwoodcottage.co.uk
www.sealwoodcottage.co.uk

1 x Grade II listed 1 bedroom holiday Cottage (self-catering)
Caravan & Camping site

The vineyard forms one element within a working farm on the edge of Linton village in the heart of the National 'Sherwood' Forest. These present owners planted the vineyard at the same time as they took on the restoration of their 18th century timber framed Hunting Lodge/Folly that was in their farm and had lain derelict for many decades.

Vineyard:
- 3.00 acres under vine
- Around m. above sea level
- Orientation
- Soils
- First vines planted in 2008
- Approximately 1,350 vines to the acre

- Sparkling wine – White
- Still wines – White, Rosé & Red

Vineyard Shop:
- **Open:**
  By appointment only
- **Guided tour & tasting:**
  Occasional Saturdays & Sundays (15.00)
- **Groups:**
  Min. 10 persons
  By prior arrangement only

Wines: Total wine production of around 6,000 bottles a year
Wine sales at Vineyard Shop & online

Winemaker: Clive Vickers (at Halfpenny Green vineyard)

SPARKLING

Sparkle – NV
- 11.5% – *Classic Method*
- Sec – *(g/lt) – Luscious strawberries/delicious summer fruit*
- Seyval Blanc, Pinot Noir

Sovereign – 2021
- 12.0% – *Classic Method*
- Brut – *(g/lt)*
- Solaris

WHITE

Celebration – 2020
- 11.5% – *Good bouquet/crisp & light*
- Riesling

Duchess – 2021
- 12.0% – *Super esthers/medium length dry end palate*
- Solaris

ROSÉ

Pink Reign – 2021
- 11.5% – *Summer fruit aromas/flavours*
- Regent

RED

Forest Hart – 2021
- 11.0% – *Smooth/rounded fruits*
- Rondo

Royal – 2013
- 11.5% – *Rounded red fruits*
- Rondo

SEALWOOD COTTAGE VINEYARD (DERBYSHIRE)

RYEDALE VINEYARDS
A member of the **Yorkshire Wine Trail**

Jon & Michelle Fletcher
Farfield Farm, Weston, York, YO60 7LS
01653 658035
ryedalevineyards@gmail.com
www.ryedalevineyards.co.uk

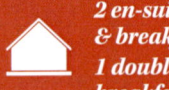

2 en-suite bedrooms (bed & breakfast)
1 double bedroom (bed & breakfast)

At a latitude of 54 North this is probably the most northerly commercial vineyard in the UK. It is now a family run vineyard that had been initially planted and operated by Stuart and Elizabeth Smith. The Smiths had been viticulturists since 1977. They then decided to expand their undertaking from just growing vine root stock when they planted the first phase of the vineyard. The present owners bought that existing vineyard in 2016 after being helping hands to the Smiths for a number of years. It is situated at the foot of the North Yorkshire Wolds and now comprises of two sites that are a few miles apart. The original site is protected by a surrounding hedge. These present owners follow a low intervention approach to the vineyard and wine making process where many activities are still undertaken by hand, including the use of an open top basket press and hand riddling, in the converted 19th century cow byre, of the original farm, which now serves as the winery. The vineyard forms part of a much larger Estate that includes orchards of rarer varieties of apple, mature woodland and open wetlands.

Vineyard:
- *14.00 acres under vine*
- *Around 75m. above sea level*
- *South facing slopes*
- *Loam/sandy soils*
- *First vines planted in 2006*
- *Approximately 1,500 vines to the acre*

Winery:
- *Sparkling wines – Rosé*
- *Still wines – White & Red*

Cider Press:
- *Sparkling cider*

Cellar Door:
- **Open:**
  All year round
  By appointment only
- **Guided tour & tasting:**
  Easter to October:
  Selected weekends (15.00)

Features:
- *Function facilities*
- *Select events*
- *Open days*
- *Open air theatre*

Wines: Total wine production of between 2,500 & 8,000 bottles a year
Wine sales at Cellar Door, at selected local stockists & online

Winemakers: Jon & Jack Fletcher
Clive Vickers (at Halfpenny Green vineyard)

SPARKLING

Royal Rosé – 2020
- 11.0% – *Classic Method*
- Brut – *(g/lt)* – *Fruity*
- Solaris *(60%)*, Rondo *(40%)*

WHITE

Yorkshire's Lad – 2020
- 12.0% – *Off dry & crisp/fresh green apple & balanced acidity*
- Solaris

Yorkshire's Lass – 2020
- 12.0% – *Aromatic & fresh/peach, melon, grapefruit & soft acidity*
- Ortega, Siegerrebe, Bacchus

RED

Strickland Red – 2020 ()
- 11.5% – *Clean & fruity/cherry & intense dark berry flavours*
- Rondo, Regent

RYEDALE VINEYARDS (YORKSHIRE)

SHEVELING WINE ESTATE
A member of the Yorkshire Wine Trail

Holmfirth Vineyard
Woodhouse Lane, Holmbridge,
Holmfirth, HD9 2QR
01484 691861
contactus@holmfirthvineyard.com
www.holmfirthvineyard.com

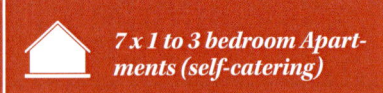

7 x 1 to 3 bedroom Apartments (self-catering)

Situated in the Holme Valley, within the Peak District National Park, this recently planted vineyard has views overlooking the surrounding rolling countryside. What had been a hill sheep farm, Holmfirth vineyard as it was originally called, was created by the present owners, Ian and Rebecca Sheveling, when they moved in.

Vineyard:
- *7.00 acres under vine*
- *Around 240m. above sea level*
- *South west facing slope*
- *soil*
- *First vines planted in 2007*
- *Approximately 1,000 vines to the acre*

- *Still wines – White, Rosé & Red*

Visitors' Centre:
- **Open:**
  All year round:
  Daily (09.00 to 21.00)
- **Guided tour & tasting:**
  Daily (10.30 & 15.00)
- **Groups:**
  By prior arrangement only

Features:
- *Restaurant*
- *Function facilities*
- *Licensed for civil ceremonies*

Wines: Total wine production of between 5,000 & 10,000 bottles a year
Wine sales at Visitors' Centre & online

Winemaker: Martin Fowke (at Three Choirs vineyard)

WHITE

Holmfirth Solaris – NV
- 11.5% – *Floral elderflower/English apples & pears*
- Solaris

RED

Holmfirth Regent – NV
- 11.0% – *Blackberries & bramble fruit*
- Regent

ROSÉ

Holmfirth Rondo – NV
- 10.5% – *Medium dry/candid fruit, strawberries & raspberries*
- Rondo

YORKSHIRE HEART VINEYARD
A member of the Yorkshire Wine Trail

Chris & Gillian Spakouskas
Pool Lane, Nun Monkton, York
YO26 8EL
01423 330716
sales@yorkshireheart.com
www.yorkshireheart.com

Camping & Caravan site
(May to October)

This vineyard has been planted within a 35 acre holding by the present owners and now forms a complete family affair. The planted area, which developed from a garden hobby planting by Gillian, has been built up steadily, from the first planting of 1,500 vines, over the years at an annual rate of up to 3,000 vines a year. The vineyard is divided into two plots, the second one being acquired in 2014, and has one of them planted east/west and the other north/south. The Visitors' Centre was built in 2017 as part of the ongoing on-site development. This flat site takes advantage of a micro-climate which can be very beneficial.

Vineyard:
- *14.0 acres under vine*
- *Around 18m. above sea level*
- *Open area*
- *Aluvial drift soils*
- *First vines planted in 2006*
- *Approximately 1,700 vines to the acre*

Winery:
- *Sparkling wines – White & Rosé*
- *Still wines – White, Rosé & Red*

Brewery:
- *Craft ales*

Visitors' Centre:
- **Open:**
  November to September:
  Monday to Saturday (09.00 to 17.00)
- **Guided tour & tasting:**
  Wednesday & Saturday:
  Summer (11.00, 13.00 & 15.00);
  Winter (11.00 & 14.00)
- **Groups:**
  By prior arrangement only

Café:
- *Themed Events & Festivals*

Wines: Total wine production of around 30,000 bottles a year
Wine sales at Visitors' Centre & online

Winemaker: Gillian Spakouskas

SPARKLING

Sparkling White – NV ()
- 11.5% – *Classic Method*
- Brut – *(g/lt) – White blossom & biscuit*
- Seyval Blanc

Sparkling Rosé – NV
- 11.0% – *Classic Method*
- Brut – *(g/lt) – Summer fruit flavours/raspberry & cherry notes*
- Pinot Noir

Sparkling Red – NV
- 11.0% – *Classic Method*
- Brut – *(g/lt) – Luscious black fruit flavours*
- Rondo

WHITE

Eleanor – NV
- 11.5% – *Herbaecous/elderflower & honey*
- Ortega, Siegerrebe

Latimer White – NV
- 11.0% – *Light, fresh & fruity/florsal aromas*
- Solaris

Wine Makers Choice – NV
- 12.0% – *Fruit flavours/rich vanilla*
- Solaris

ROSÉ

Latimer Rosé ()
- 11.0% – *Sweet red summer fruits/ fresh acidity*

RED

Eleanor – NV
- *Black cherry/low tannin & mellow acidity*
- Pinot Noir, Cabernet *(?)*, Gamay

Latimer Red – NV
- 12.0% – *Black plum/blackberry & spicy flavours*
- Rondo

Wine Makers Choice – NV
- 12.0% – *Black plum & spice/vanilla*
- Rondo

YORKSHIRE HEART VINEYARD (YORKSHIRE)